WELCOME
TO MY
PARA"NORMAL"
LIFE

EXIE SUSANNE SMITH

First Edition August 2012

ISBN-10: 0692414002
ISBN-13: 978-0692414002

DEDICATION

To my husband and son. Thank you for the gift of time, supporting me at every turn, the gentle nudges to finish, and loving me as much as you do. I am a lucky woman.

Thank you to my mom for teaching me to love books and to my dad to love words.

Louise thanks to you for being my language arts guru and for pushing me to carry on.

Thank you Chris for being my one childhood friend that understood what I meant when I used the term "gut feeling". For being just as curious as I was about the subjects of intuition and life after death. We were weird little kids!

ACKNOWLEDGMENTS

Cover Art

Kate Cowan of KC Designs

FORWARD

Before you start reading my paranormal journey, there are a couple of matters I would like to clarify for you. Wanting an easy flow for my book, I chose to group similar events into chapters. With this format, there are time gaps between like events within the chapters. For the purpose of clarity, I placed the symbol "###" as a divider between each individual event.

Something else I would like to make clear is what I mean when I write, "I do or have done research." I started to look into the psychic and paranormal subjects when they became a part of my world. I read everything I could get my hands on in order to help me understand this new aspect of my life. I also wanted to assure myself I was all right, both mentally and physically. Early on, it was difficult to find reading material in these areas. The local library might have had just one book on these subjects. I did find a couple of books at used bookstores and even went into a store that mostly specialized in occult goods. In both places, the books I purchased were more about astrology. I learned that you are "when" you were born. Although I did not understand it at the time, this research would help me in the years to come. People carry traits from their astrological sign. This knowledge has been incredibly helpful, entertaining and true. I also researched in, and read from, other forms of publications such as newspapers and magazines. In these types of publications, the subject matter was typically written about close to the celebration of Halloween. Over time, I have witnessed great changes in popular thinking and beliefs on these subjects.

Cable television has also helped me with my research. It has brought to life both ghost and paranormal shows, some even science based. These shows often give me starting places for further research, the proper verbiage and in some cases they helped to verify several of my personal events. I have found that the greatest source of information is the Internet. Every imaginable aspect of these subjects is now available to research. As a caution in your own research on the Internet, make sure your information is from a reputable website and that you double check everything you find.

It has been amazing to feel free and confident enough to come out of hiding from the psychic/paranormal closet. I hope that by writing down my experiences, I can help clarify some topics for you and possibly lead the way to a more open conversation on the subject matter. It is an amazing and diverse topic.

INTRODUCTION

My eyes are open to the view of my bedside clock. It is 1 a.m. I am wondering why in the heck I am awake. As the grogginess starts to fade, I notice the darkness of my room. My bedroom door must be closed. But, I never shut my bedroom door. I always see the soft glow from the hallway nightlight in my room. I do not like, or feel safe in, total darkness. I am completely awake now and conclude that the sound of my door closing is what woke me up. I am extremely attuned to noises and sounds. I know instantly where a noise or sound is coming from. It is a safety mechanism. My stomach is now flopping with fear and I get a sudden, strong feeling that I am not alone in the dark. Ever so slowly, I roll onto my back from my side and try to get a look around the room. With my vision still adjusting, I feel that keeping my eyes mostly closed, open only to slits, is a good idea. I start scanning the room from left to right. As my eyes pass over the closet, my inner alarm tells me something is in there. My bathrobe is usually hanging on its hook and will sometimes make itself resemble a scary monster shape. But, not this time. This time I know the hook is empty. My robe is draped over the railing at the foot of my bed. I start telling myself, "Simply reach out and turn on the bedside lamp," but I can't move. I am too scared. My eyes, still masked in slits, never leave the closet and the shape just inside. I keep trying to make sense of what I am seeing. It looks like a long figure or maybe that it is wearing something long, like a cloak. I think cloak because it looks like it has a hood on its head. I can barely see facial features because of the deep shadows but what I can make out is not pretty. It is grotesque. Still telling myself to move but can't, I am frozen with fear. Out of nowhere comes a wee voice in my head, "Talk to God."

So I did! I didn't think that starting this conversation would cause this monstrous figure to glide toward me but that was the result. I ask again, out loud this time, "God, please protect my soul. Be with me and give me strength." The figure then glides backward to where it was originally. As it traveled to the back of the closet, it disappeared. Lunging for my bedside lamp, I turn the knob with a click and the room floods with a calming, familiar light. Feeling a bit more safe, I get out of bed to inspect the closet. Nothing, there was nothing to suggest that anything had been there. I do not know what I expected to find, maybe that creepy character had an odor or perhaps it left an imprint in the carpet. I open the door to the hall and slide my desk chair in front of it.

Getting back into bed, I went over everything that had just transpired. I must say, I was surprised at the voice in my head telling me to converse with God. I had not been raised in an overly religious family but it felt like the right thing to do, the right person to ask for help. I laid back on my pillows and decided I should say a proper thank you. So, I did, out loud, while staring at the ceiling. I went back to sleep, with my light on, of course. I think I handled things pretty well, for a 12 year old kid!

Welcome to My Para"Normal" Life!

CONTENTS

CHAPTER 1

MY GIFT

Being able to see, hear and sense spirits is something I am honored to say is a part of my life. I have been bestowed a special gift. I see my gift as two parts. First, it is a gift from God and second, something that was passed through family blood. My dad had an imaginary friend as a child. Fifty years later, he and I were discussing my gift. He asked about the ghosts or spirits, as I refer to them, and how they appear to me. I gave him several different descriptions from different sightings and he laughed. A bit taken aback by his reaction, he touched my hand in a loving gesture. He then said, "Oh my God! All these years I thought my childhood friend was a figment of my imagination. He wasn't. He was a ghost. Holy cow!" It was now my turn to laugh. As our discussion continued, my dad explained his conclusion and, for the first time, thought about how the imaginary boy was dressed. He said that because of the way he was dressed, he was probably part of a previous family that lived in their 100 year old farmhouse. My mom also has some abilities and senses things. I would say she has some psychic ability. My mom's sister had the same abilities but a bit stronger. Getting this much ability from both sides of my family explains to me my gift and maybe even why my abilities are stronger than any of theirs ever were.

Psychic and paranormal subjects were not talked or written about back when I was a kid. It was a shock to find out not everyone felt or saw things like I did. Thank God, over the years, the subject has become less taboo and more accepted. With the Internet, television shows, and the many books published on the subject, it is not as shocking or odd anymore. With that said, I do feel odd sometimes. I find it interesting that even close friends and family members will ask me if I have seen any ghosts lately while they roll their eyes and snicker. It is so cut and dry for them. What they cannot see or feel does not exist, period. I humor them mostly, but occasionally I don't. I might say to them, "Funny you should ask, there is a spirit standing right behind you!" I know it's probably not very nice but the look on their face is worth it.

I am not exactly sure when I started to consider these abilities to be a gift. To be honest, for many years it was a burden, not a gift at all. Once I got past being frightened by it all and recognized the physical feelings that happen when a spirit is around, I considered it to be a cool gift. It was, and still is, a learning process. The way I see my gift now is with a continually educated eye. People are now paying attention to what I have to say. They are willing to listen when I speak about it scientifically and proficiently because I am educated on the subjects. I find the paranormal and psychic worlds fascinating and would miss my gifts if they went away.

My research and education has taught me that I have the following abilities: 1) Clairaudient, a person who can hear what other people cannot, like voices; 2) Clairvoyant, a person able to see and perceive things clearly that other people cannot; 3) Prophetic Dreamer, a person who dreams of things in whole or part that become future events; 4) Psychic, a person who has extra sensory perception (ESP). Recently, I have added being a "Sensitive" to my list of gifts. A sensitive is someone who can perceive information psychically (ESP) and is susceptible to attitudes, emotions and the feelings of others. I have felt fights, stress, anger and upset emotions from other people my entire life but did not think twice about the fact maybe not everyone was able to do that. Now that I have educated myself on the topic of being a "sensitive," I can confidently state that some emotions I feel come from other people. Recently, I was in the car coming home from an appointment when a funeral procession passed by me going in the opposite direction. One car toward the end of the line stood out to me. It seemed to zoom sideways toward me. Right after that feeling surrounded me, I burst into tears. I sobbed. I remember thinking, "What the hell is this and why am I crying?" As the car continued by, I just as suddenly stopped crying. Amazed by my reaction to what I assumed had to have come from one or all of the passengers in that car, I went home and did some research. I found the term "sensitive" and it fit. This could also explain why I am not a fan of huge crowds. They exhaust me because there are too many mood swings for me to take.

So far, my gifted life has been an amazing journey and I would not change a thing. It is who I am, who I have become and who I will continue evolve into being. I will be shaped by this gift for the rest of my life.

CHAPTER 2

DWELLINGS

I want to take you back to my childhood home, in particular the basement. That is where I found journals of mine that date back to ages eight through twelve. Reading those journals again, I realized what spooky old memories that basement still holds for me. Whenever I was in the basement, there was always the distinct feeling that someone was there, unseen, or that someone had been standing there seconds earlier and just walked away. It always felt as if my every move was being watched and I knew that eventually one of the times I went down there, something or someone was going to reach out and grab me.

Our basement had two sections. There was a finished section that was a walkout, with a gaming area, lounge area and a laundry room. It was a wonderful family gathering space. It had large picture windows and a door to a deck that sat privately in the woods which backed up to our house. The other side of the basement, separated by a wall and a door, was not so wonderful. This section was unfinished with a bare cement floor, cinderblock walls, tiny slits for windows, and the entire area was piled high with a ton of unused family treasures. Very little natural light made it into the space because of the tiny windows. It was dark and shadowy in the daytime and pitch black at night. The only easily accessible light was just outside the door to the unfinished area but it didn't cast light more than

about a foot into the darkness. That might have been
all right if I didn't have to go another foot past that
shadowy light to reach the pull cord to illuminate the
unfinished room. Holding my breath, I would take a
huge step through the doorway into the dark and grope
around for the string pull cord that hung midair. The
cord went up to the ceiling and across the room. It was
strung on two squeaky, old pulleys to a chain. It was
attached to a bare bulbed fixture in the center of the
room. I would panic if I hit the cord with my hand but
the light did not come on. I then had to grope in
midair, in the dark, for the cord. I never felt more
vulnerable in my life. Many times from upstairs, (my
bedroom was directly over this part of the basement), I
would hear the squeaking of the pulleys and the clicking
of the light turning on. Of course, I was home alone.
The only way those pulleys squeaked was if someone
was physically pulling the string that runs through
them.

Just once, in all the times I heard them squeak, did I get up enough courage to tiptoe to the landing, look around the corner and down the basement stairs to see the doorway into that area. I wish I hadn't. The backroom light was on and I knew it had been off earlier. I know that because I passed the doorway to the unfinished section of the basement after getting a game out of the finished section. I remember wanting to scream but nothing would come out. My instincts had me run to the bathroom. It was the only room in the house with a lock on the door. I locked myself in and waited for someone to come home. Moments after I locked the door, I could hear someone coming up the basement steps. The sound of footsteps seemed to stay only in that area. They never reached the landing or kitchen just beyond. I will revisit this phenomenon in another chapter because the sound of the footsteps did not stay on the stairs much longer.

###

Having now lived away from my childhood home for over 22 years, I wonder what I would feel going back in that house. In particular, what would it feel like to be in the basement again? Nothing did ever grabbed me (thank God!) but I did hear shuffling sounds and saw movement out of the corner of my eye. I did not know as a child that I should be crediting those events to spirits. Now, I do. At the time, I thought it was my vivid imagination, but it was not. In fact, because of the knowledge I have gained in the years since, of spirits, the paranormal, and of myself, I am convinced that something did dwell in the basement of my parents' home particularly in the basement. I now feel that whatever was there was attached to the land, not to me or to the house. My reasoning has to do with the woods behind the house that ran for several miles.

One of the many days I spent playing in those woods with friends, we stumbled upon the ruins of a settler's cabin. It was not far from my parents' home. I had learned about the Native American tribes that lived and

traveled through the area and about the history of the

town. I was not surprised to find the relics of a cabin

and stone fireplace in our midst. When all of this

knowledge is combined, it begs the question, "Was the

spirit activity around me as a kid a result of these early

settlers or the Native Americans? Unfortunately, for

now, that question goes unanswered. Perhaps someday

I can gain access to the house again and solve this

mystery.

Eventually my parents moved away from my

childhood home and into a condominium. Since they

were downsizing, they needed to get rid of some of their

belongings. They decided to hold a yard sale and asked

me to help. The perfect warm weather day arrived and

our work began. This seemed to be taking forever and I

was very unhappy about it. I had hoped they would be

more prepared but they were not. On one of the many

trips into the basement area, I asked my spirit guide, "Please help me have patience and understanding." Not feeling any calmer and still going up and down the stairs to retrieve things, I stomped back into their basement to get another load. With that load in my hands, I turned and took a step up on the bottom stair with my left foot. The heel of my right foot lifted off my flip-flop, but the flip-flop didn't budge. It stayed down on the floor. Turning and looking down, I was certain I would see my dog's sweet face laughing up at me with her paw holding down my flip-flop. She wasn't there nor was anyone else. My immediate thought was my spirit guide was doing as I asked of her, "Slow me down!" I thanked her for getting the message across to me and went back to work; slower, easier, and nicer to be around.

CHAPTER 3

HEARING TIMES TWO

Being able to hear footfalls in my childhood home was the first evidence that I am clairaudient. This means I have "clear hearing" or the ability to hear voices, sounds or music not audible to the normal ear. I hear spirits two different ways. I hear them in my minds inner ear and with my actual outer ear. Because I hear a spirit, or other noise, with my outer ear does not mean that other people will hear it. The story that follows is an example of hearing with both my inner and outer ear.

###

After many years of having to be up and out of the house every single morning by a certain time, I had a period of several months where I did not have to be anywhere early in the morning. I was no longer working outside the home and our son had a driver's license and his own car. Thank goodness because he was a swimmer on his high school team. He had to be dressed and on the pool deck at school by 5:15 a.m. My plan was to enjoy a week or two of freedom from an alarm clock before getting back on a schedule. It had been a lovely week of alarm clock avoidance until I had an appointment that required me to set an alarm. This plan went awry, as plans can. I was awakened by an odd noise some place in the house before my alarm ever had a chance to go off. Dazed, I sat up in bed and tried to figure out what the sound was, where it came from and what time it was. I swung my feet over the side of the bed and checked out the clock. That is when I noticed I had not set my alarm, after all. The noise that I heard, that subsequently woke me up, was within five minutes of the time the alarm would have gone off.

I never figured out where the noise came from or what it was. I thought all day about how coincidental the noise was that woke me up that morning. I do not believe in coincidence so denial is thy name. That night, I asked out loud to no one in particular, "Would you please wake me up in the morning at 7 a.m.?" I did not set my alarm and went to sleep. The next morning I woke up very startled to the sound of footsteps in the hallway just outside my bedroom door. I lunged out of bed and was ready to protect myself. I was supposed to be alone in the house. I rounded the corner of the bed and noticed the time on my husband's clock. I stopped in my tracks! In bright red numbers, it read 7 a.m. I thought to myself, all right smart ass, now say thank you. Okay, so it happened once, actually twice, but would it happen again? That night I asked again to be awakened at the same time, 7 a.m., and off to sleep I went. It seemed like only minutes had passed when I clearly heard my name being whispered in my ear. It was 6:50 a.m. The day after that I was again awakened at 7 a.m. This time I was awakened by my cell phone ringing from over on the nightstand. I know it rang. The dog woke up, too, and the face of the phone lit up the dark. When I checked the incoming phone log later that day, it showed that it never rang that morning.

For the next two weeks, I used my "spirit alarm clock" with great success as an amazingly on-time wake up service. I started to feel guilty for imposing on the spirits and stopped asking. For those two weeks, the spirits were accurate within 5 minutes every single day. They finally settled on the method of waking me up by walking in the hallway outside the bedroom door. It worked great.

When the spirit wake up service started, I was excited to gain a new aspect of my gift. My childhood journals reminded me of how I used to hear footsteps on the basement stairs. This was not a new occurrence in my life. Apparently, I had taken this scary childhood memory and stuffed it into the back of my mind. However, I was not scared anymore. I realized that no one was here to harm me, only to assist me upon my request.

A simple shopping trip with my son turned into more than just that! We left the mall, got into our car and started to back out of our parking spot. We realized there was not an exit in the direction we were heading so we had to go around the end of the row to get out. Not understanding why they set up the parking lot this way, we were discussing better solutions as I drove. Suddenly I heard a voice yell, "Sue, look out!" Noticing just in time, I swerved to the right and just missed a paneled service van that was accelerating backward out of its parking spot. It seems the driver of the van was not paying any more attention than I was. I was thankful someone was paying attention and chose to warn me. I said, "Son, that was so weird. I heard a voice tell me to look out."

He said, "That is weird. I wondered where your super human reflexes came from!"

The voice was very clear and centered at the top of the inside of my head. At least that is where it registered. It was like a tingle in the top, back part of my brain. The sensation was inside my skull. I was so pleased to have avoided an accident and happier still that I had heard a warning voice in my mind. I said to myself, "Thank you to the heavens, to whoever had been kind enough to help keep us safe." I wondered if it was my spirit guide or guardian angel. I said to my son, "I should get one of those key chains that says, never drive faster than your guardian angel can fly." He laughed.

After that, I began hearing spirits more and more with each passing day. I was happy that my gift seemed to be growing and evolving.

###

What happened next has great meaning to me and was cool as hell. Our dog, Lola, and I had just taken laundry into my bedroom to put it away. She hopped up on the bed for a quick nap and I continued talking to her as I put clothes into my dresser. A bell rang. It was the sound from the kind of bell you have to pick up and swing back and forth so the clapper inside makes contact. The clanging noise came from out in the living or dining room area. I spun around, away from the dresser. Lola was already up on her feet and facing the door. We looked at each other and simultaneously headed out of the bedroom. We stopped just short of the group of bells sitting on my desk. I felt a bit apprehensive. Without touching them, I looked at the desktop area, checking to see if any of them had been moved. There would be a dust ring. I am not a real committed housekeeper. They all looked to be where they should be and the dust was not disturbed. I had a feeling I knew which bell actually rang but I had not heard any of their tones for years. I picked them up one at a time and I rang them. The sound from the brass southern bell was the one we had heard. This was my grandmother's bell. She would ring it when she needed something during her bed-ridden illness. When I rang it, Lola came hustling over, stopped at my feet and stared up at me. "Aha, I am not crazy," I said aloud. "Nice to get confirmation, even if only from the dog." I thanked my grandma for letting me know she was visiting and told her I loved her. My grandma and I were very close. It meant so much to me to hear that bell and to know she was around.

CHAPTER 4

DIZZINESS EXPLAINED

My cousin and his wife had just had their first baby. Like any good family member, I invited myself over for a visit. They lived just south of a city I love, Washington, D.C. With great excitement, I booked a flight and flew into Ronald Reagan Airport. I always have to sit on the left side of the plane. The reason is the incredible view but I will fully explain later. My flight day arrived and I boarded the plane. I got settled into my seat, ordered a cocktail when available, had a bit of conversation with my row mate and then settled back in anticipation of one of the coolest approaches in to any airport. The view is majestic. As we started the approach for a landing, our plane dropped in over the Potomac River. The captain came on over the intercom and told us about the view. He did not want us to miss it! I think they drop in over and follow the river to help cut down on the jet noise. Whatever the reason, thank you! We had the best roller coaster ride and an amazing perspective of some major historical landmarks plus we saw a bit of beautiful Georgetown University. Everything was fine until the plane suddenly veered from our river course and passed over the runway. We suddenly touched down. I was thrown for a loop at how fast this happened. I thought maybe the cocktail had upset my equilibrium or maybe my sinuses were messed up because my head was spinning. I was very dizzy. Maybe all those things, combined with the excitement of seeing family members, were throwing me off. My row mate noticed and asked, "Are you all right?"

I realized I was clutching the armrest so hard my

fingers were white. I let go of the armrest, smiled at him

and said, "Yes, well, or I will be once we reach the gate

and stop moving, thank you!"

To my relief, the spinning in my head finally stopped

by the time we reached the gate. However, my insides

were rattled. This event had scared the hell out of me! I

have never felt such a violent, spinning sensation. At the

time, I felt as if I was going to be sick but I do not

normally get motion sickness. I had thought, maybe it

was my aunt that had passed away. Maybe she was

coming to greet me. That was just wishful thinking and it

did not make sense. This was something else. I had to

calm down for the time being. My visit was short so I

had to put the confusion aside and enjoy my family visit.

After two marvelous days in D.C., I flew home without

incident. I was glad to see my husband and son. During

the drive home, I told them what had happened during

the landing in D.C. They commented about being able to

tell I was still upset at how violent the sensation had been. Both of them were sweet and offered up some very plausible explanations. I guess they thought I was looking for a rational answer. I knew inside that what I felt was not a normal reaction. I have flown for years and landed at airports dozens of times. I have never had any reaction, let alone one so violent. There was a reason I had been so affected by the landing and the answer would someday find me. Again, there was a need for me to put it aside and get back into the swing of things at home.

Days passed by and I would catch myself replaying the landing in my head. One day, while on the floor stretching after a workout, I was subconsciously running the landing through my mind again. This time using a different scenario I was concentrating on what was outside of the window. The answer was not in the plane so I looked to the outside or, more accurately, to the area surrounding the airport. In my mind, I looked off in the distance. I see a bridge. Out loud I said, "Bridge, bridge, oh my God, what bridge is that?" I pulled my laptop onto the floor where I was sitting and I searched the Internet for plane crash information near Washington, D.C. I remembered a plane crash in that area several years ago that was absolutely horrific. I also remember being very emotionally affected at the time of that crash. There it was on my computer screen. Back in 1982, Flight 90 had crashed into the 14th Street Bridge. Not believing it I said, "That can't be the same bridge!" The flight had been trying to take off during a blinding snowstorm. The plane clipped the bridge with its landing gear and crashed into the Potomac River. Sadly, 74 people on the flight were killed and another 4 people, sitting in their cars stuck in traffic on the bridge, were also killed. I was blown away. I truly did not expect to find any information on the Internet about that immediate area. At the time of the crash, the news story had been all over the television. If you saw any of the news feeds, you would never forget it because it was heart wrenching.

All these years, I thought the crash had taken place much further up the Potomac River. The close proximity was a shock. Did the crash site and my violent dizzy spell have anything to do with one another? What if I did make the leap and put these two events together? What was the cause of the dizziness? Maybe it was only the sensation of the river giving way to the land. The plane seemed very low and almost as soon as we came over land, the wheels bumped the ground as we landed. I was trying to explain away the sensation but couldn't, not completely.

I got on the Internet and searched for possible explanations of the dizzy, spinning feeling I'd had. Was it vertigo? With this you can have a "dropping away" sensation or as it is called, the "carnival ride effect." I knew what vertigo was like because I had been affected by it years ago. I was so dizzy I could not even hold my head up without getting sick to my stomach. I ruled out vertigo. Another possibility was an inner ear infection or maybe that my ears had not yet adjusted to the cabin pressure of the flight. Having lived a lifetime with ear problems, I ruled this one out from experience. Finally, the last explanation I considered was a possible spiritual event. Not understanding what was meant by "spiritual event," I searched for it by typing in "dizzy feelings and spirits." This brought up information on paranormal phenomena and spirit manifestation. I read on and found more information about "feeling dizzy." This can be a classic sign that a spirit or spirits are around, trying to manifest, and I perceived it. I also read that the dizzy feeling comes on quickly. I agreed with that. It further stated that spirits need energy to manifest. The electromagnetic field they then give off can cause dizziness. Not everyone, it said, feels this but some people are sensitive and do. I did not make the leap yet to either believe I had felt a spirit trying to manifest or that I felt the energy from spirits at the crash scene. I consider it as another possible explanation for my sudden and extreme dizziness. It would be a while before I put this event and a past dizzy spell spirit manifestation together. I later realized that I am sensitive.

No matter the cause for that feeling, what I did and where I did it brought back the memory of a horrible accident and all those associated with the plane crash. I prayed for those that lost their lives, for their families, for those that survived and for those who witnessed it. God bless them all.

CHAPTER 5

VISITATIONS

When I was young, I thought my life mirrored every other kid's life. I truly did not consider the fact that other kids were not hearing strange noises and seeing shadows move around the house. This is the kind of stuff that was not talked about in public, so I didn't. Only on occasion was this discussed, in the privacy of our home, of course, and then we used the word "gut feeling," never anything else. Ignorance was bliss as far as others were concerned. For many years, it made me feel left out on my own most of the time, especially in social settings. It was "stay quiet or become an outcast." Maybe I would even suffer testing by a doctor or, even worse, possibly be institutionalized. Besides, when you think of a haunted house, you do not think of one that is only ten years old. Haunted houses are supposed to be old Victorian types, deserted, dilapidated and rotting.

Not being able to talk about what was going on meant I had to keep my feelings bottled up. I could sense situations around the house and at school because I knew more than I should. This made me feel awkward toward those people and my own family. I was a mess and that made me an outsider. My whole life was a mess but I could not seek help in a friendship or professionally. I was afraid to talk about what I was seeing and hearing. I could not risk a friend telling someone and the professional would probably have me put away or forced to take psychotic medications. Things got worse when my main confidant and much loved grandmother died. I simultaneously hit puberty. Puberty seemed to have had a marked effect on my abilities. They increased. Not only could I see shadows moving and hear basic thumping and bumping sounds, I now heard voices, too. It was not clear conversation, rather, indistinct murmurings that I knew were voices talking in sentences. I had no idea that years down the road, the nondescript murmuring would become clear, understandable words and conversations. Something else was new. Remember the footsteps I talked about on the basement stairs? That used to stay confined to the stairs. I could now hear them all over the main floor of the house. Bedroom doors started to open and close. Also, something that struck me as funny started happening. Our dining room wooden chairs would creak as if someone had just sat down in them to eat a meal when dinner had been over for hours. At least it had been for the living occupants of the house.

In the midst of all these psychic changes and new happenings, my aunt came for her annual visit from Washington, D.C. I loved when she visited. We always had the best conversations and she was easy to be with.

During one of our talks, my aunt unexpectedly asked,

"What's up?" She said, "You're acting different from last

year." I laughed at that and had to wonder how someone

who saw me so rarely could know me so well. I knew I

could tell her everything that had been going on and she

would not rat me out to my parents or laugh at me. In

fact, she did as always, listened with rapt attention

without passing judgment. Her reaction was pure

excitement for me. She was surprised by the stories but

believed me and believed in me. It felt great to get

everything off my chest. I had been hiding so much and

wanted to tell someone for a long time.

She asked, "Do you know what the term "spirit

visitation" means?"

I knew what she was talking about and replied. "Do

you mean like Harry Houdini? He had said to his wife

that he would come back and visit, if at all possible, after

his death."

"Yes, exactly!" she said. This line of conversation was scaring me but was buffered by her next comment.

"Since I am quite a bit older than you, I know I will die first and will do everything in my power to come back to see you. And with your gift, you will know it when I do." We laughed, hugged and moved on to other topics.

This conversation did not come to mind again until years later when my aunt came for an unexpected visit. She informed us she was terminally ill and had a very short time to live. Talk about devastating news! She was going to die. How could that be? The night before she left to go home she sat me down. "Susie, do you remember the conversation we had years ago about spirit visitation?" I threw myself into her arms and listened while she explained. "When I die, if at all possible, I will come back to see you and say goodbye." I knew that if anyone could do it, my aunt damn well would! She was a very strong woman. We kept in contact until it was no longer physically possible for her to do so. Her march toward death became a slow slide as the cancer dragged her painfully away.

It was during the spring of 1981 and my mind was on college finals. I was studying like a mad woman, trying to make up for a few sporadic transgressions during the semester. One evening during a homework cram session in my efficiency apartment, I was all set up in the middle of my bed with papers and books everywhere. My senses came alive. It was literally as if someone had flipped a switch. I became dizzy. The room seemed to be swirling and the café curtains that hung from the two windows suddenly blew up and out from the rod. The room became icy cold. In an instant, it became clear to me what was going on and why. My brave, wonderful aunt had passed away. She was indeed coming to say goodbye, and with gusto. Tears filled my eyes, ran down my face and rolled over the huge smile plastered on my lips. I had so much love in my heart that I thought it was going to burst. I started to talk out loud to her. I said, "YOU

DID IT!" I repeated that many times. I was in shock at what was happening, not shocked that she had actually done it. I said to her, "Houdini's got nothing on you!" I kept talking and told her, "I'm so proud of you. I knew you could do it." The room was still ice cold and seemed to be swirling. I was so dizzy. The curtains were no longer standing straight out but moved like the windows were open and a breeze was coming in. This was so crazy and happening in my tiny apartment bedroom. I thought my neighbor might be pounding on the door any second wondering what was going on. She never did. I continued to talk to my aunt, "I love you and I'm so glad you don't hurt anymore." Then I asked something I have always wanted to know, "How does it feel to fly?" At this point, I am not sure how, but I knew she was running out of time. I said, "I'm sorry you suffered so badly and that I wasn't there by your side at the end but I kind of am anyway. You're free, Auntie, YOU'RE FREE." Crying even harder now, I told her, "I love you. Thank you for coming to see me. This was fantastic. I knew you could do it! I will love you forever and see you again someday…thank you."

The room slowly stopped spinning and the temperature returned to normal. I was personally a long way from being back to normal. I was in shock. What the hell had just happened? My aunt had given me a most precious gift, several in fact. She used her time and energy to come say goodbye to me and she had proven to me that I do have a gift. There was no longer room for speculation or denial. I was smiling still. How could I smile when there is death involved? This brought a new perspective for me about death. This event showed me death is not the end. While the physical body withered and died, my aunt's soul continued on. The shock wore off and I realized I was still sitting in the middle of my bed. Everything was quiet. Normally, the television volume was loud, there was traffic noise outside and I could hear noise from my neighbor's apartment across the hall. Now, there was none of that, just stillness. Looking down at my hands that laid limp in my lap, I found it odd how still they were. I thought they might be quivering, as my insides were. I also wondered how long this had lasted. I glanced at my bedside clock. Only a few minutes had passed even though it seemed much longer. Turning and putting my legs over the edge of the bed, I reached for the phone on other side of my clock. I knew it was going to ring. I also knew also it was going to be my dad. Bringing the receiver up to my face, I said, "Hi Dad."

Normally, he would have asked if the phone had even rung. It hadn't and he didn't. He did not even realize I had answered the phone saying his name. He and I would talk about this all at another time. For now he was hurting because he had just lost his only sibling. He said, "I'm calling to let you know your aunt has passed."

I said, "I know Dad, she was just here. She did it Dad, just like she told me she would. It was amazing." He thanked me for letting him know and said it helped him feel better. We talked for a few more minutes. I told

him, "Dad, I'm sorry for your loss. I love you, and I will

see you in a few days." We hung up and I cried. I felt

alone and left behind.

.

Keeping with the theme of family visits, this next event

is about a family member I had never met. I was in the

kitchen getting dinner started when my husband yelled

from the other room, "See you shortly." He left to collect

our son from swim practice at the high school. When he

left, I was at the sink peeling potatoes. This put my back

to the kitchen entryway which is no big deal, normally.

However, this time I had a sudden, overwhelming feeling

that I was no longer alone in the house. We live on a high

traffic road. There are interesting looking people that

walk by on the shoulder of the road which leads in and

out of town. On occasion, our old garage door would

shut but not stay shut. I was thinking maybe someone

thought the open door was an invitation and had

wandered in. I glanced sideways and spotted a paring knife laying on the counter. With my right hand, I reached out and grabbed it. My senses were telling me whoever had come in the house was getting closer. I could not wait any longer. I simultaneously spun and jumped around to face the entryway while doing my best banshee yell and brandishing the paring knife. I surprised the spirit I caught him

peeking around the side of the refrigerator. All I could say was, "Oh!" and the spirit's eyes seemed to say the same thing before he was quickly gone. I fell back against the counter and felt relaxed now. I let the air I had been holding in gush out. I smiled and thanked him for coming to see me. With a shake of my head and some rapid eye blinks, I thought out loud, "Who the heck were you?"

He had appeared in a very deliberate way; grainy, like an old photo. He had a hat that looked to be from the 1940's or 1950's and the cutest, simplest grin on his old, handsome face. Talking out loud again, I said, "Thanks for the visit but you scared the crap out of me. I'll bet you're having a chuckle over my yelling and leaping about, whoever you are." My husband returned from picking up our son. I could hardly wait to tell them both what had happened. They were excited I had a spirit stop by but mainly their interest was dinner.

Several days went by and I still did not know who that was in my kitchen. I kept repeating out loud, "The visit was amazing, thank you, but please help me figure out who you are." Forgetting about the spirit visit for awhile, I did some chores around the house. I also had some computer work to do so I headed toward my desktop. I walked past the cupboard where I keep my family history research. It hit me like a ton of bricks! There is a picture in there that I need to look at right now! I sat, with a thud, in front of the cupboard door and started to pull out my files. I knew exactly which one I needed. I found it and yelled out, "Ahhh, I found you!" I was looking at a picture of my great-grandfather on my mother's side. He had appeared to me like he had been cut right out of this picture; same brownish gray graininess, same hat, and same sweet smiling face. I turned my face to the ceiling and yelled out, "I know who you are!" This is the only picture I have ever seen of him. If he had not come back resembling it, I would not have figured out who he was. My mom and I had been talking about her parents and her grandfather just the week before. I think that is the reason he showed up. We had been talking about him and my mom did say he was a character. She told me that he had liked her very much so maybe he came to pay his favorite granddaughter's daughter a visit. His visit to see me was extraordinary, touching and made me feel very special. When I told my mom about it, I recalled the look on his face. I don't think he had planned on me seeing him which made it even more fun for me.

The following weekend, we went to a famous pottery house in Detroit where I found, and purchased, a tile that reminded me of my great-grandfather's face peeking at me. It now hangs in my kitchen on the other side of the entry way and refrigerator where he was trying to spy on me. I have said to him many times, "Thank you for paying me a visit. I am sorry we missed each other in this lifetime but I hope to see you in Heaven someday."

There was personal validation in this event. I now had to admit to myself that I am clairvoyant. I had a feeling someone was there, trusted that feeling and was rewarded with a visual from my great-grandfather. By definition, I sensed him by using a means other than the known senses.

It was Christmas time. For me it is always a time of year that brings on strong nostalgic urges. These urges can play out in many ways; family, gifts, gift wrap, decorations or food. My husband was pleased, this particular year, because the urge was for foods from my childhood. That meant baking and cooking for days at a time and it was well worth it. Finally, after a couple of weeks, everything on the cooking list was prepared, except for my grandma's double yeast cloverleaf rolls. They are not hard to make. You just have to get the science of it correct. The yeast has to activate. I had not made these wonderful rolls in a few years so I was a little nervous. For me, this was the most important recipe of all the nostalgic foods I was preparing. I'm not sure why, but I thought what the heck, and asked aloud if my grandma (Gma, as I called her) would please come and make her roll recipe with me.

I proceeded to get all of the ingredients together and proof the yeast. Everything went together easily. It was now time to turn out and knead the dough. Again, I asked for Gma's help. I couldn't remember the technique or the kneading time. The recipe instructions were hard to read. I started in and had a cold chill run down my spine. I thought that was odd but kept up my steady pace. It was a much easier process than I remembered

and chuckled to myself saying, "Honey, you look like a
pro!" I was still chilled but figured I would not be after
kneading the dough for a few minutes. When I finished,
I turned slightly to my left to grab the greased bowl I had
prepared for the dough to rise. Further to the left was a
microwave oven. While glancing into the glass front of
the microwave, I noticed an outline of a person right
behind me. I turned quickly to see what that was about
but there was nothing there. It scared me. The thought
crossed my mind that maybe I was throwing a shadow. I
did not see how that was possible. The light over the
work surface would have thrown the shadow down on the
cupboards rather than at head level and directly behind
me. It should have been angled off, shorter and at least a
foot behind me. I turned back to recreate the exact stance
and movement but there was no shadow directly behind
me this time. Doing all the movements again, for a third
time, I could not recreate the outline of a second person
in the microwave glass. What had I just seen? Did I

think someone was there? Do I want to believe someone was there? Yes, I do. I believe that Gma was there, spending time making bread with her granddaughter.

Thinking deeper about my experience while I cleaned up my mess in the kitchen, I noticed I was no longer chilled. I had issued her a personal invitation to spend time with me and to do something in life she loved, which was to make bread. After so many years of getting feelings just like this one and denying them, I think it is time I stepped up and acknowledged my gift. I now know when a spirit is present. I just have to be brave and admit it. I cannot validate this event by a photo, recording or any other witness. I have to add here that I think some events are private moments, only for one person. I think they are chosen by the spirit to be that way. This time I had requested a visit, which she could have ignored, but did not. I was able to spend time with a woman that I admire, love and miss. She would want me to believe in myself and to know that what I feel is

real. I do, finally.

CHAPTER 6

GAMES OF CHANCE

As I have stated before, I get feelings about people, places, things and situations. I learned during my college years that I get feelings about cards in a deck. There was a drinking game, before beer pong, called "Red-Black." It had simple rules. The group sits around a table with a beer in front of each person. One person has a deck of cards and asks each person at his or her turn, "red or black?" You state the color you think the dealer will turn over and if you are wrong, you take a drink. The turn moves to the person seated to your left. As I said, simple and effective for most because everyone wanted to

consume beer and get drunk. The goal for me, most of

the time (which no one at the table ever knew) was to see

how many times I would guess correctly in an evening.

Then I started to guess the other players' cards, too. I

took advantage of every opportunity to exercise my

senses. I was correct at least half the time and sometimes

much better. I loved the feeling I got when I tuned in. It

was as if my brain got a tickle and then I would see a

picture of a card. It was either red or black. The cards

always seemed to come up as a queen, in my mind, but

rarely was it ever a queen. That did not matter to me

anyway for my experiment, and to be honest, guessing the

suit never crossed my mind at that stage. The tickle

feeling in my brain eluded me when there was a large

crowd either in the room or at the table. I would still get

some attempts correct but I think that was more luck of

the guess than a feeling.

The other thing that affected the percentage of card colors I got correct was the beer itself. The tickle feeling was dull, or nonexistent, if I had more than a glass of beer. What I saw was a sheer curtain or veil and the card was just behind it, unreadable. I thought that was very telling. Alcohol affects the brain in more ways than people realize.

Years after college and having left drinking games like Red-Black behind me, my husband and I took our first trip to Las Vegas. Walking into a casino for the first time was like stepping into an explosion of bling in amounts that I had never seen before. The first thing I did was to go right to the adult version of Red-Black, better known as Roulette. I was ready to play but my level headed husband put a hand on my shoulder, and said, "Maybe we should observe for a few minutes so we can see what the game is really about." We watched for awhile. He commented to me, "From what I see, this game has some bad odds against the player." After watching for a bit, it was obvious he was right but I still wanted to play. That would happen later.

The casino was a steady dull drum of noise in my head during the day. I did not know how that would affect the tickle of my senses. I had no idea, yet, how loud and wild a casino became at night or how different it would feel to me. We toured around, hit the pool, had some drinks and then went to the room to get ready for the evening. The elevator bell announced the casino floor, the doors opened and a wave of frigid air mixed with incredibly loud sounds and spikes of emotion hit me right in the face. BAM! The noise of the machines was through the roof. Add the lights and the jam of people, it was totally overstimulating to the senses. We got the lay of the room and looked at machines and table games. I found a Roulette game but the table stakes were too high for a beginner. Well, too high for this tight wad. We learned that the table game stakes went up at night. That was too much for me so I just watched and learned more.

Walking in and around the slot machines, I wanted to see if I could get a feel for a machine. I know it sounds silly because they are cold machines. I did have a bit of luck picking a machine that "felt good." I did not win big money but enough to buy cocktails by the pool.

I did finally get to a Roulette table the next day; less crowed, less noise and better prices. I was successful with the red or black choice but could not pick a number to save my life. I netted about $37, had a blast and bought us lunch in the casino.

A girlfriend and I used to enjoy what we called a "girls weekend" once a year in Niagara Falls, Canada. We visited vineyards, drank wine, shopped, gambled and relaxed. Before dinner, we would visit the slot machines in the casino. She would laugh because I would walk along the slot machines to see if one called out to me. She would walk along with me asking, "What are they saying? Do they call your name or tell you things like your hair looks marvelous tonight?" I mostly ignored her, although it was funny, but I had to concentrate. Deciding I would sit down at a machine, I knew within a couple of plays if this was "the machine." I would either stay or move over one and play until I would win enough to cover cocktails, dinner and maybe even dessert. Again, I was not out for the big bucks, I simply wanted to cover my needs for the upcoming evening. I hope the next time I try to enter a casino, I am allowed in!

The card games and casino events helped me further understand that I needed to trust my feelings and instincts. I had to let go and relax.

CHAPTER 7

SPIRITED SPIRITS

Sunday evening, 6:30 p.m., cold, windy and pitch dark

outside. It was Michigan in December. Today was one of

those days that had me chilled to the bone. I could not

get warm. When this happens to me there is only one

thing to do. Immediately after dinner I get into pajamas,

climb into bed with a hot cup of tea and pull up the

down filled comforter. My son knocked on the bedroom

door and came in. He was checking on me but laughed

at me instead. I must have looked funny with the covers

pulled up to my nose. He plopped down on his dad's side of the bed and decided to watch television with me for a bit. I do not remember what the show was we were watching but something funny happened. I turned to look at him and caught movement behind him. The smile on my face faded as I observed a male spirit that I could see through. He walked through the bedroom door, continued straight ahead about three feet to the treadmill and faded away just as he reached it. The spirit was almost robotic in his stiffness. His arms were stiff, straight down by his side and he stared straight ahead as if in a trance. I scared the hell out of my son when he witnessed my reaction to what I had seen. He then turned to look to his right to see what I was looking at. I inquired, "Did you see that?"

"Did I see what?"

"A male spirit," I said, "well, three quarters of one anyway. He faded away at about the knee. He just floated into the room and then faded away just as he got to the treadmill." The spirit looked to be in his 30's with a full head of dark brown hair. He was wearing a red polo shirt and light colored pants, maybe beige. I was sad that my son did not see him because I thought maybe he might have recognized him. I did not know who it was.

My son said, "That was new!" I laughed at that statement but he was right. There was a new spirit in the house. Later, as I turned out the light to sleep, I asked if my spirit guides would please help me figure out who the male spirit was that had appeared for me earlier. I am still not sure who the spirit was but he has appeared at different times in other locations of the house.

About seven to ten days after his first appearance, he appeared in a couple of my dreams. Since that event and those dreams, I have had a phone conversation that confirmed who this visiting spirit was. Because of the extremely delicate nature of the conversation, topic, and the person I conversed with, it would not be proper for me to give more detail. The person I had the conversation with confirmed for me that the spirit came to me because he knew I would be talking to this person, eventually. I think the spirit also knew we would figure out the connection together. God bless them both.

During yet another night, I was all snuggled in bed, sound asleep, when something woke me. As usual, I needed to know what time it was and checked the clock. I tried to get a grip on what time it was and hated the fact I had been disturbed. I felt something walk across the top of my pillow, right above the crown of my head. It was not the heavy clomping of a person, but something light, like from my childhood when our cat would walk across my pillows. It was oddly more comforting than creepy so I rolled over and went back to sleep.

I love to catch Lola watching spirits move about the room. It is amazing to see. For me, there is no other explanation than the fact that she, too, sees spirits. She is totally absorbed by the activity and her head moves back and forth like she is watching a tennis match. Most of the time, I cannot see what she sees. All I see is her sweetness totally absorbed by the invisible activity in front of her.

Since we are talking about Lola, I will share this event now. She was a bit scared and surprised, just as my husband and I were, when this happened. It was around 2:30 a.m. when Lola woke up with a full body jolt of all 20 pounds. It was so strong that it shook the whole bed. Through half opened eyes, I raised my head up ever so slightly to watch her. I observed as her whole body physically snapped up off the bed. She landed on all four feet and continued facing the foot of the bed. She added a low, fierce growl. In all the years we have had Lola, she has never reacted this intensely to anything nor had we ever heard that vicious of a growl out of her. Both my husband and I are were wide awake but not moving. I asked him, "Did you hear anything, like a door or movement?"

He said, "No."

There is a window at the foot of our bed which was opened just a crack. Maybe it could have been noise from outside. However, Lola's steely glare fixed about a foot and a half to the right of the window. Slowly, she rotated her stance and glare to the left of the window. Now she concentrated on the far left corner, still growling fiercely. My husband was trying to calm her down by petting her and talking nicely but nothing was working. He held her and tried to calm her down but she did a maneuver that sidestepped his attempt. She was not taking her eyes off whatever this was. My husband said jokingly, "I think one of your ghost buddies is here."

I turned to look at him and said, "Yes, I do, too!" He was not sure he liked that I agreed with him. I continued, "Everything is fine. None of the spirits that come around us are here to do harm or they would have done so by now." I reached out for Lola and put my hand on her still ridged back. In a quiet voice I told her, "Hush, it's okay." As I patted the bed between my husband and me, she settled back in. I was surprised she listened but thought it was a good sign. I said goodnight to them both and leaned back against my pillows. I left my eyes wide open in the darkness. It did not take long before I caught sight of a black mass in the shape of a human head and shoulders. It rose up about four feet in the air from the corner of the foot of the bed. It eventually blocked out the light on the cable box under the television which sat on the dresser.

I spoke softly and told this dark shadow, "Please go away, you are not welcome in our bedroom ever and right now we would like to go back to sleep." Once I spoke, the shadow started to ever so slowly sink out of sight. I said, "Thank you."

My husband said, "Really? You're polite, at what is now 3 a.m., to a ghost?"

I said, "Of course, and it's a spirit not a ghost."

I then rolled over to find sleep. My request seemed simple but I knew tomorrow, when I had the house to myself with the spirit, we were going to talk and it might not be infused with politeness. Before I found sleep again that night, I remember thinking it was odd for our son's spirit to show up in a place it had not before. I wondered why. I woke up in the morning with no more answers than I had the night before as to what that event was all about. At least I knew what I was going to say to the spirit at some point during the day. I thought I recognized this shadow spirit. I have seen him many times and he has never changed his shape. I thought it was my son's spirit or the spirit that has always been in his room and around the house. That might explain why I was calm the night before. Since our son had gone away to college, I wondered if the reason the spirit came to me was because maybe he wondered where my son was. We had moved him into his college dorm a month earlier and he had come home only once since.

After breakfast, I went down to my son's room, stood in the center of it and started to talk out loud. I was hoping the sprit would hear me. I asked him if he were questioning me about our son. I told him where he was and that he would be home in a few days. I also told him that he would leave again and be gone for several weeks and that this routine would continue until spring. I must tell you I cracked up thinking, wow, if people could see me now, they would have me committed! Continuing to talk to the spirit, I told him he was not allowed in our bedroom and to please stop scaring Lola as he had. I will admit this event had a level of creepiness to it. This conversation thing was new to me.

Wrapping up our conversation, I said to him, "Have you given any thought to the fact that there might be people in Heaven waiting for you to show up? They might be missing you, and, in fact, God might be missing you, too." Now for the big finish. "I think you need to move on and go home to Heaven."

I thought it would have been all right to wait a week for my son to come home so they could say goodbye to each other. In case that was too long to wait, I told the spirit he could go to our son's dorm room to say goodbye. I made a mental note at that point to call my son at school and let him know he might be having company and to warn his roommate.

I stood still and remained quiet. I wanted to see if the spirit would show up or make a noise but he didn't do either. I was left wondering if he listened or thumbed his nose at me. Time would tell. A month went by and no shadow figure appeared to my son or me. It was exciting to think that I had done a good deed. I sent him on to Heaven. This was the first spirit I had helped cross over. Exciting, right? Life was moving on and I figured we no longer had a haunted house. Thinking that way gave me some mixed emotions, but bottom line, I missed him. As it turns out, I did not have to. It was only a day later that we had company again in our bedroom at night. This time I think I awoke on my own. For some reason, I had moved way down low in the bed and was flat on my back. This was not my normal spot and I never sleep on my back. Being so out of place, I wondered where Lola was sleeping. Usually, she is tucked into my side but she was not there. I was actually sleeping on the spot she normally slept. Glancing up to my right, there was Lola, way up at the head of the bed in between our pillows, leaning up on her front legs like an Egyptian sphinx. She was calmly lying there with just her head moving from side to side. She was watching something move at the foot of the bed. The cute expression on her face made me smile. She was not anxious, just watching. I glanced at the area at the foot of the bed and did not seeing anything. I shifted back up to my regular spot. While moving up in the bed, my right foot was roughly smacked twice, on the very top of my toes. I turned to see if my husband was indeed sleeping and still in his spot. He was. And, he was not playing a prank on me. I was checking but knew darn well the taps had come from on top of the covers. I could not see anything but had the distinct feeling it was the spirit who was usually around my son. I also had a feeling that he was either bored or pissed off. The first emotion I had was happiness. Our spirit was still here and Lola seemed to have adjusted to him. The spirit, however, was angry. What I picked up was his attempt at scolding me for trying to send him away from home. He is happy here, damn it! It hit me as interesting the way I picked up "home" from him, not his or ours. I did say out loud, "You can stay in our home but stay out of our bedroom. The rest of the house is open to you. By the way, I'm glad you didn't go."

My husband then spoke in a groggy voice and said, "Are we all happy now so we can get some sleep?"

I am strangely happy to report that the spirit is still here. He has never returned to our bedroom and I have not again tried to send him home. I think we found a

footing and are keeping to it. I can understand this was

his house before ours. We let him have some space but

made sure he understood that it is our home now.

Not all spirit activity in our home happens after dark.

This next event proved that fact. Lola and I were sitting

on my bed. I was on the edge of my bedside cleaning out

a dresser drawer and she was stretched out in the center

but toward the foot of the bed. I shut the drawer and

turned to say something to her. I noticed how tense and

alert she was. Her ears were fully forward and her back

was stick straight. She then started to growl deep in her

chest. My senses came alive and I knew there was

something to the right of me, but I could not see it.

Looking back to Lola because her growl got more intense,

then back to where she was concentrating her attention,

in the exact spot she was looking, the air rippled. The air

literally rippled like water does after you drop a rock into it. I blinked my eyes fast several times but it was not my eyes. The air had actually rippled. The energy in the room changed at the same time. It felt as if something had unfolded from a crouched position on the floor. It rushed toward me a few feet, backed off just as fast and then disappeared. I knew it was gone. That area felt empty now. I do not know who or what it was or what it was about. Whatever it was, I had the feeling its intention was to get in my face to scare me. This can be looked at another way. Maybe I scared it and this was its reaction. Either way, I surprised this energy mass first by seeing it and, second, by not being scared by it. This was a first and, I admit, confused the hell out of me. Later that week, I watched a paranormal show on television. The host stated that people with psychic gifts are like a beacon in the dark to spirits and they are drawn to us. The attraction is similar to the way moths are drawn to light.

###

Long after I wrote this chapter, I had the opportunity to talk with some psychically gifted people. Our conversation came around to shadow people. It was interesting to learn they think shadow people always appear in a similar shape. They believe them to be only dark and have a human shape or outline with no details (facial features, clothing etc.). This freaked me out because the shadow person that had recently appeared in our room seemed to be the same one who is always around. But, he felt different to me. I am now questioning if it was him or not. It would explain Lola's strangely aggressive reaction to a shadow that should have been familiar to her. For me, further research on the subject of shadow people is necessary.

CHAPTER 8

PETS

Our first "doggie daughter" was a 23 pound Schnauzer named Bailey. She had attitude, and on occasion, a good one. Bailey loved my husband as if she was married to him but only tolerated me. I am glad to say our relationship changed as she got older. We became closer and in her last few months of her life we were great buddies. When she passed away, we laid her to rest with a family funeral service in the garden under our bedroom window. I missed her terribly in the tearful months that followed. The house felt empty but not for long. After 14 years with Bailey, I was quite familiar with the noises she made while rambling around the rooms of the house. I remember the sound of her toenails clicking on the wood floor and seeing her walk down the hall. I cannot tell you how long I continued to hear those sounds in the house after her death. It registered to me one day that I had just heard dog toenails clicking on the wooden, kitchen floor and then I saw Bailey walking down the hall. I stopped believing I was hearing and seeing her "out of old habit" and admitted that she was here in spirit form. I hoped she had come home to stay.

###

My husband gets up at an awful, early hour in the morning for work and is sweetly careful not to wake me. One morning as he headed to the bathroom, which is across the hall from our room, he decided to shut our bedroom door on his way out. His kindness backfired as my old "closed door phobia" struck. I woke up to the sound of the door clicking shut. As I lay in bed, the room started to spin around. It made me dizzy. I propped myself up on my elbows, seeking relief. It did not help so I tried blinking my eyes and looking around the room. I thought that might bring things back into focus. That was also not effective so I tried to focus on the curtains. They, and the room, had a beautiful glow from the full moon shining down. The glow carried onto the white down comforter on our bed. I tried then to focus on that. I caught movement. There was not anything visibly moving. However, when I was looking at the bed, there was something invisible moving on the comforter. It was leaving indentations as it moved around. What I saw next blew me away!

The comforter scrunched down into a perfect circle. It was exactly like the circles Bailey made when she curled up and laid down on the bed with us. The circle also formed in the exact area she preferred to sleep. Honestly, once I figured out what I was seeing, I was fine with it. In fact, it touched my heart. What did not sit well with me was just beyond Bailey's spot on the comforter. There was a second indentation that formed at the foot of the bed. It was "U" shaped like the imprint of a human's butt and legs in a sitting position. I threw the covers back and scrambled over the top of the bed. I hustled into the bathroom and almost mowed my husband down! After I apologized, I grabbed his hand and dragged him back into our bedroom. He had to see the indentations for verification. I flipped the light on and pointed at the two spots on the comforter. I told him everything that had happened from the minute he got up. He was very patient and understanding, maybe he even believed me. I was fine, however, even if he did not. I knew what had happened and felt honored that Bailey wanted to cuddle up with her mom.

The spinning was still so new it did not dawn on me what was happening. The current thinking from the paranormal field (which I believe) is that spirits use energy from the surrounding area to appear. This can make a person who is sensitive feel dizzy or ill while it is happening. This was knowledge, unfortunately, I did not possess at the time of this last event.

We have never had a cat. I like cats but we are dog people and currently have our wonderful doggie daughter named Lola. She is a rock star in the neighborhood with the kids because she is so darn funny, lovable and laid back. Whenever I get a sensation of a spirit in the house with us, I watch her reaction to see if she can either see it or hear it. Turns out Lola, like her mother, is getting accustomed to having spirits around. At first, Lola was frightened because she did not understand what was happening. Generally speaking, she is now comfortable and certainly entertained by them.

Occasionally, a spirit seems to bother her. I am not sure if it is human or animal but I do not think it is mean spirited. I would be very upset if I thought she was frightened and I would not stand for a bully spirit in my home. I do remember a time when Lola came running down the hall to stand behind me and peeked back around my legs like something was chasing her. Thinking that I completely understood what was going on, it pissed me off and I let the spirit know. I raised a fuss, out loud, about what I assumed was bad behavior on the part of the spirit. I told it to stop or it would have to leave. I left the situation at that. All spirit activity chilled out for several days. I sort of felt bad for casting a broad net across for all spirits, both animal and human, but I felt worse for Lola. They had rousted her off the couch from a sound sleep. Things were better for her after that.

###

Our son was home from college over a semester break so he was fair game for household chores. I had him vacuuming in the living room while I was down the hall cleaning the bathroom. When he started up the vacuum (or "carpet eater" as we think the dogs look at it) I heard toenail sounds crossing the kitchen floor and then in the hall outside the bathroom. Lola hates the vacuum so I was ready to offer up words of comfort to her when she came to me for safety. She did not come. I watched as she trotted past the bathroom door and headed toward my son's room. I laughed and figured she thought it was safer to be further away from that mean carpet eater. Our son finished the vacuuming and shut it down. This usually signals an "all clear" and Lola comes out of hiding. After a few minutes, I thought it was strange she did not come out of his room. I got concerned and headed there to comfort her. As I approached the room, I started talking out loud with comforting mommy words. I stepped into his room and looked around, she was not there. No way had she walked back past the bathroom without me seeing her. She must have, but to be sure, I went looking for her. I found my son and Lola together back in the living room. He asked, "What's up?"

I asked him, "How did she get back out here so fast?"

He said, "What do you mean? She never left the room, been in my way this whole time. Trust me on this!"

I said, "Yes she did. I heard her toenails on the wood flooring and saw her walk by the bathroom door. I looked right at her." He simply shook his head, no. I said, "It looked just like a flesh and bone living dog." He looked at me with a glint in his eye. I said, "No way was that the spirit of Bailey. It couldn't have been."

He looked at me a bit longer, finished wrapping the cord up to the vacuum, and walked away mumbling, "When is she going to learn? She can see spirits."

I have to admit to myself finally that I do, in fact, see spirits. Why not admit it? I have had this ability for over 30 years. I admit that I still find there are some things I am skeptical about and one of those things are orbs. To me, they are easily explained away and/or disproved. Often times, it is just dust which was stirred up by someone entering a room. The dust floats in front of a camera and you have an instant orb. Another way an orb appears is when you are outdoors and get a great shot of a bug that happens to fly in front of the lens. I am a cynic on this subject and will be until I see it for myself. There is nothing wrong with wanting and looking for more proof regarding an event. Just because something happens, does not automatically make it paranormal. Sounds good anyway, until something happens and there is no other way to explain it, no matter how hard you try.

I had been listening to the television and doing paperwork while sitting on my bed. I was comfortable and cozy. My eyes were feeling gritty so I knew it was time to turn in. I changed into pajamas and turned out the bedside light. I reached forward for the covers. There, right in front of me, was the most amazing thing I had ever seen! It was a perfectly shaped circle floating in midair. I could not take my eyes off it! It was floating just above the bed. This thing, this ball shaped object, was about six inches in diameter. At first, it was just suspended in space but it gently started moving sideways. This was unreal! It was so much to take in and it had a beautiful reflective glow. I thought maybe the glow was coming from the light of the television because that was the only light source in the room. The circle floated slowly between Lola and me. We were in my bed. It was interesting to me that she, too, had noticed the ball and was following it with her eyes. I wondered if it were merely dust, would it hold Lola's attention this strongly? What about the glow? Since when is simple dust iridescent? I continued to follow its movement across the bed until it became undetectable just before it reached the closet. Looking back at Lola, she did not seem overly impressed. She had been acting unsettled just before the circle appeared but I did not put two and two together right away. It makes sense, in hindsight, that she had unsettled, nervous behavior. She has reacted the same way, in the past, to paranormal experiences. I would love to believe this was an orb. I have been talking about them for years but never thought I would actually see one. I do think it was an orb but I cannot prove it. I do not have any photos and only a dog for a witness. I will wait anxiously for the opportunity to see another object of this kind and will then have something for comparison. For me, this is just the beginning of my journey to answer the question of whether I believe orbs are real or not.

I pray every day in the shower. I started this because it was the only time of day I knew I would get total privacy. So, it's not weird, just practical. I pray to Father God, Jesus, Mother God, spirit guides, angels, family, friends and pets. Yes, I said I pray to Mother God. I think I was made in her likeness. We have more than one spirit guide in each of our lifetimes. Also, during our lives, spirit guides can change. There might be a different guide that is better suited to serve or help us during whatever is happening at that time in our lives. Angels are with us always but will not step forward to help unless they are asked by us to do so. I have been told by several psychics that I am surrounded by strong women from my family but they, unlike an angel, are not always there. It is believed that they are in Heaven to continue to learn but come to us when we ask. I also believe we have many pets through our many lives and they, too, go to God. Not everyone believes that our animals go to Heaven or to God. I do. I also choose to honor them and their unconditional love by talking to them and thanking them for their love and companionship.

One morning while I was praying, I felt sentimental. Without giving it a thought, I invited all my pets to come and visit me. Immediately a dizzy feeling came over me but I did not connect the two events yet. I thought maybe it was the heat and humidity of the shower that was getting to my sinuses. Once out of the shower and dressed, I noticed Lola acting very odd. She was roaming around the house and could not seem to find a place to lay down for more than a second. Several times she would sit or lay down, only to jump up and rush off like she had been poked with a sharp object. Her ears and tail were down. She was not her usual, happy self. She seemed to be almost in a panic. Her odd behavior went on for roughly 20 or 30 minutes before I realized what was happening. I had given permission to ALL my pets from ALL my past lives to come and visit, never dreaming they would show up all at once. I stopped what I was doing and noticed the house was full of energy.

Laughing at myself, I apologized to Lola, "Little one, sorry, I messed up. I'll fix that." I continued, "Sorry, but I have to ask you ALL to go, you're scaring Lola and this is her home time with me." Within minutes, the high energy feeling was gone, along with my dizziness. Lola was no longer trying to find a safe place to lay down. She simply flopped onto the floor where she stood and fell asleep with a huge sigh of relief. I thought to myself, "oops!" but how in the hell would I know that would happen? I waited around for a moment to make sure Lola was the lone pet in the house. I then went to my bedroom where I had some clothes to put away. When I finished that chore, I turned from the dresser and took a couple of steps toward the door. WHAM! I became incredibly dizzy. I reached out, grabbed onto the bedroom door and kept my head bent forward to try and stabilize myself. My attention was caught by a swirling mass of air near the bedroom door. The swirling motion took on the appearance of a whirlpool. This was in midair. From my research, I figured out this was a mass of energy from a spirit trying to materialize. I watched as it took on the shape of a cat. It became a perfectly formed cat out of what looked like a milky cloud of white mist. The cat walked to the door and rubbed its way around the corner as it left the room. It stepped out into the hallway and looked back at me over its shoulder. With its tail straight up in the air, it gave me a condescending look that only a cat can give. The misty cat took a couple more steps forward and then gently evaporated. I had a vision flash of this cat as orange and white striped. I am not sure how but the vision was clear as day. In this lifetime, I have had several cats but never one in this house and never an orange and white one.

With the misty cat's grand exit, pet visitation ended. My dog, Lola, was relieved. Actually, seeing the energy manifest and the "cat of mist" were both new events for me. I loved every minute of it.

CHAPTER 9

PARANORMAL WITH A TWIST

I have a girlfriend who also has a psychic gift. She is someone I talk openly with regarding spirits, intuition and perception. She recently moved close to me and invited me over for a visit. After a tour around her house, we sat down at the kitchen table. It sits in front of a big window that looks out over her beautiful backyard. As we were talking and sipping some wine, an hour passed. Into the second hour, I finally asked, "What the hell is outside this house?"

With her fist, she hit the table and gave a shout, "Ha, I knew I wasn't imagining it! I knew something was here and if anyone could see it, you would!"

It was the oddest thing. Whatever it was, it stayed just out of sight, on the outer edge of my vision. The only thing I know for sure is that it was solid black. I asked her what she was seeing. She said, "I'm not sure. It doesn't show up really. It stays around the edges of the house and I think it's black."

I agreed, and she felt better, sort of. I said, "I'm getting the feeling of a raven or a huge crow with an immense wingspan. It seems to be circling close but cutting its flight pattern back just out of our view."

She said, "Exactly."

We sat and sipped in silence for a few minutes, and then I asked her, "Do you sense anything?"

She said, "No."

I sensed something but it was just outside and I did not have a good feeling about it. Inside the house, my senses picked up that everything was fine. She decided, as long as the inside was good, she would leave things alone. I understood that but silently hoped "leaving well enough alone" was a good plan.

About three weeks after the event at my girlfriend's house, I was at home, doing some journaling on the living room couch. I caught movement out of the upper portion of the left picture window. This same movement repeated itself several times. I was a bit freaked out. It looked just like what I had seen at my girlfriend's house. The movement repeated a couple more times and then stopped. I have never seen anything like that here before and, to date, have not since. As far as I know, a black mass is still being seen around the outside of my girlfriend's house. In fact, about three weeks after I wrote this section of the book, she came to our house for dinner and informed me the movement was still happening. Her boyfriend had also witnessed it. She said, "He jumped up from the kitchen table where we sat by the window and ran outside to see what the hell was flying around the house." She continued, "He came back in confused because there was nothing there."

The next event is related to the last only by the small fact that the action was in the living room of my home. I thought this event a bit weird, but funny. My husband is not the least bit inclined to think it funny, only weird. Our living room is set up with the television against the wall. To the left of the television is a window and then a door out to the deck and side yard. Our couch is across from the television, about 12 feet away. Right behind that is a small walkway and then the wall behind is lined with shelves and our desktop computer. My usual spot on the couch gives me a view of the window. At night when we watch television, it is dark so the window becomes a black mirror of sorts. You can, however, still see outside. For at least a week, maybe longer, I had been seeing something move past the window outside. It looked like smoke or fog. One night, I sat up to check the lake for steam. The water might be warmer than the air but I figured it was probably smoke from a nearby bonfire. After seeing this white mist for the third or fourth time, I got off the couch to investigate the possible origin. Our neighbors have many bonfires so I thought I would find it was their smoke coming our way. No bonfire. In fact, no one was outdoors, at all. Night after night, the white smoke or mist showed up and I kept getting up to see if I could figure out what it was. Finally, my husband asked me, "What is going on out there? What are you seeing? You keep popping up to look out the window."

All I said was, "Nothing, I guess I'm seeing things."

The next night I saw it again and asked my husband, "Did you just see something go past the window?"

"No," he said, "but I'm not really paying attention because I wouldn't expect anything to be in our yard this late at night."

At this point, I tried to rationalize what was going on. Maybe it was headlights on the road from a passing car, a reflection off the house, fog off the lake even though it has warmed back up. I know I am not crazy! I am seeing something. Or, maybe someone is playing a trick on me. I decided to ignore it. I am done playing this game. With dramatic relish, I put my arms up in the air over my head as if I needed the momentum to get up off the couch to go shut the blind on the window. The shocker happened when my arms were in the air. The white, smoky thing went by the window at the same time. What I saw blew me away! Because my arms were in the air, how I now saw the smoke changed my perspective. It hadn't been going by outside at all. It had been inside the whole time and going by behind us while we lounged on the couch.

In the telling of this event, I refer to what I saw as smoke, thinking that is what it was. I would otherwise refer to this as a mist. By definition, a mist or spectral mist is an energy field that looks like a cloud, mist or haze. There may or may not be a certain shape or color to the cloud, mist or haze. Thickness, density and consistency can vary, also.

The next events are also on the topic of reflection. However, my reactions were very different. The first event took place while I was standing at the bathroom vanity drying my hair in the mirror. The mirror picked up the reflection down the hall, including part of the foyer and the back door. On the wall beside the back door, I hang seasonal, homemade, quilted banners. There was a quilted Halloween "Boo" banner hanging up at this particular time. I made it years ago but still think it is cute. I glance at it while using the mirror. This particular day, while doing my hair, I had the sudden and distinct feeling of being watched. Using the mirror to look down the hall, I glanced at the banner. I was stunned by the fact that in the banner was a pair of eyes staring back at me. Those eyes were looking directly into mine. This was horrifically shocking and intense. My arms went limp and fell to my side. All I could do was stare back. Managing to find words, I said, "I'm fine and I'm going to be fine," and with that the eyes were gone. As I have stated before, I get impressions in my mind. They flash in and quickly disappear. This impression was of the same grotesqueness I saw when I was 12 years old. It was like that image I saw in my closet, at my parents' house. Out loud, I said, "Checking up on me? Well, you lose! I am even more God's child than I was back then, so bug off!" This gave me strength and when I knew my legs would hold me, I went to the banner, took it off the wall and looked it over. I did not see anything out of the ordinary. I hung it back up and went back to the bathroom mirror. I wanted to recreate what I saw but I could not even come close. I wanted badly to disprove this event. I thought I was done with this creep from my past. I had not thought about it in years and I am amazed that it can still affect me so strongly.

The second event happened about two years ago. I had worked during the day, filling in for my mom at her job. Occasionally, she needs me. I got home, we had dinner and I was trying to sneak in a load of laundry. Next to the laundry room is the back door where I can see our small, side yard. I have a garden in that area and love to admire the blooms through the window of the door. However, having lost track of time, it was dark out and I could not see my flowers. As I was turning to walk away, my attention was drawn to the right side of the door's window, to the right of my shoulder. I noticed the low light from my son's room behind me reflected into the window. Included in that reflection, I realized, was the face of a man. I was home alone and this reflection meant there was someone standing in my son's room, about two feet behind me. I reacted with a dramatic, 180 degree

Exie Susanne Smith

spin of my body and arms but I found myself looking

into an empty room. Thank God.

Chapter 10

THE PASSING OF FRIENDS

When our son was a newborn and even into his toddler years, I was constantly exhausted. I do not have a single spiritual journal, no quick notes, not even personal paranormal stories from those three years. Honestly, until this next event, it had not dawned on me how spiritually disconnected I had become.

###

The phone rang. It was a good friend of ours with news that his wife was gravely ill. She had been taken to our local hospital and was now unresponsive and in the Intensive Care Unit. This is a woman we called friend but even more than that, she and our little boy had a very

special bond of love for each other. Several days passed
with no update on her condition. That was
understandable, her family was not leaving her side. We
were worried sick and our son kept telling us he wanted
to go see her. We told him she was in the hospital but the
rules did not allow him to visit at such a young age. I am
embarrassed about this next part. Today, I would know
better than to be so rude and intrude like I did. I drove
to the hospital, went up to the ICU area and lied to the
nurse at the desk. I said I was her sister so they would let
me see my friend. I walked into her room and felt that I
had intruded upon her husband and their kids. I humbly
apologized for intruding and backed up to leave. Her
husband, always a kind and gracious man, told me to
come over and visit with his wife. I went directly to the
bed and touched her hand as I talked lightly to her for a
moment. I then politely left the room.

I rounded the corner and walked away from the ICU.
I slammed myself against the wall, leaned forward at the

waist, put my head between my knees and tried not to pass out. My psychic abilities had come roaring back, completely unexpected. It rocked me to my core. The instant I touched my friend's hand there was a connection and feelings were passed between us. It almost knocked me to the floor. I could not get home fast enough. I needed to hold, and be held by, my family. I charged into the house, scared both my husband and my son, scooped my son up off the floor and walked into my husband's arms. While he held me and calmed me, I told him what my psychic impression was about the person I had just been to see. I could not use her name because our son would understand who I was talking about and that our much loved friend was now gone. Our son wiggled to get down. He had been held long enough. This gave my husband and me the chance to finish our conversation, code free. I told him about going into the room, touching her hand and being bowled over with spiritual emotion. I knew in an instant that she was no longer earthbound. We both hoped and prayed that I was wrong but I knew I was right.

The next evening we were chatting and clearing up after dinner. I had just gone back into the dining room area from the kitchen when I sadly got confirmation that our friend had indeed passed away. I turned my head and looked over my left shoulder at my husband. While commenting on something that had been said, suddenly, a hand appeared and gently touched my shoulder. Sucking in air from the shock of what I was seeing immediately got my husband's attention. I heard him ask, "What's wrong?" I was too busy taking in the perfection of the hand, the skin tone, the slenderness of each finger, the nails, all perfect and all with a soft white glow. Just as suddenly, she took her hand away from my shoulder and was gone. She went up through the dining room ceiling.

I heard my husband ask me again, "What's wrong?" I lifted my eyes back to his face across the room and he asked, "What did you just see? Your eyes got huge while looking at something on your shoulder and then you turned your head and followed something up to the ceiling. Are you okay?"

I told him, "Our friend was just here to say goodbye. She has passed." My husband sank back against the kitchen counter, with sadness on his face. Not more than a few minutes had passed when the phone rang. It was her husband telling us in the saddest voice I have ever heard, "She's gone."

My husband had answered the phone and said, "We know. She was just here to say goodbye. We are so sorry."

This was an incredibly sad event. We felt awful and our poor son, just a toddler, cried for days for her to come back to see him.

The following Christmas, our son, now three and a half years old, opened the box our tree topper angel is stored in and shouted out our departed friend's name. My husband and I almost cracked heads trying to simultaneously look into the box. We realized for the first time just how much our friend resembled the angel. Fourteen years later and we still refer to our Christmas angel topper by our dear, departed friend's name. It is very special to us.

People come and go from our lives, in ways as different as the people themselves. Some stay longer than others do. This can be good and/or bad. The one constant in all of it is WHY they stay. I believe they are with us for our education, our life's education. We are here to learn, after all. An example in my life of a person coming and going is one particular girlfriend. We have been in and out of each other's lives many times over the last 40 years of our friendship. Years ago now, we had just been reacquainted after a separation when her wonderful father sadly passed away. He had been dealing with failing health for years but that did not lessen the pain of his death. He was her dad and her rock. I hurt from the loss, too. I loved him like a second dad because of his huge capacity for caring. The funeral was rough on my friend. It was not the time or place to reconnect with her or to have much of a conversation. I waited a couple of days after the funeral and then reached out to her by phone. The first thing she said was, "Sue, I'm hurt my dad hasn't come to see me."

I told her, "Relax, he will. We don't know for sure what goes on after you die. Maybe there's an orientation or something!" I was sort of kidding about the orientation and just trying to calm her down in hopes that his visit still had time to happen.

Later that day, after our phone conversation, I had the feeling someone was in the house with me. I asked, "Who's here?" With that acknowledgement, something appeared in my peripheral vision, just down the hallway and in my laundry room. What I was seeing seemed to be the side outline of a black figure. It was leaning back against my washing machine. An image of what this spirit was wearing popped into my mind. Gray slacks. A golf sweater. A blue cap. The shadow person stayed in my laundry room for three days before it hit me. It was my girlfriend's dad. I asked out loud for confirmation, "Are you my second dad?" I knew inside that it was him and said, "You need to go see your youngest daughter. She is confused and hurt that you've not gone to her." I left it at that and went about my day. I thought that might get him to go see her. The next morning while having coffee, I looked down the hallway and he was still here. In my mind, I knew he was still here because his business was not done with me. Otherwise, he would have left already. I cannot explain how I knew, but what he wanted of me came into my mind. I answered his question and said out loud to him, "Don't worry. I will look after your daughter for the rest of my life." With that, his shape faded from the laundry room and the feel in the house went back to normal. The energy charge had vanished.

Within a couple of days, my girlfriend called so excited she did not know where to start. I started it for her and asked, "How did your visit go with your father?"

She said, "Sue, my dad came to see me. Wait, what did you say?"

I said, "Oh nothing, go on."

She then described his clothes, "He was wearing gray pants, his golf sweater, oh, and a blue cap!"

I was stunned, to say the least. We talked for a few more minutes. I asked one last question and we hung up. My last question was, "Why the sweater and the cap?"

She said, "He always wore a sweater and a cap because his heart was bad. He was always cold."

I didn't know that as a kid. I knew he was sick and always wore a sweater. She called me later, after dinner, to make sure I was okay. I guess I was really quiet during our last phone call. I told her that the description of his clothing was exactly what I saw on the spirit in my laundry room. It was now her turn to go quiet. We had talked days earlier and I had told her there was someone hanging around the house. It then dawned on her that her father had come to see me first and was hurt by that. I told her not to be. He was looking for assistance from me and then he felt free to go to her. I told her what he wanted from me. She said he told her when she and I were kids that he hoped we would be friends forever. He always knew we help each other to be strong.

Several years ago, a beloved neighbor abruptly became ill. Within a few days, he passed away. Before we found out the sad news, I noticed the appearance of a black figure, indoors, toward the back part of my house. I could tell it was not our son's spirit. This apparition was not the same height and not the same shade of black. I did not know black mass spirits came in shades. Evidently, they do. Seeing a "shadow person" made my stomach sink. I had a bad feeling about why it was here and who it might be. I called my husband at work to warn him that I thought our neighbor had passed. He was confused and thought I had gotten a phone call with this information. I said, "No, not a phone call. It was my psychic line calling."

All he said was, "Damn."

Later that same day, I was walking through my living room and glanced outside across our lawn. I noticed movement over on the neighbor's lawn. There was a likeness of our neighbor floating up the yard toward the house. He was wearing blue jeans and a white business shirt with the sleeves rolled up to the elbow, unbuttoned at the neck, with a white tee shirt on under the business shirt. He looked great! Perfect, in fact, literally perfect. There was a white haze over him to soften and complete his angelic appearance. I blinked and he was gone. I called my husband at work again, telling him the extremely sad news. I called our son out of his bedroom and told him, too. Just before dinner that evening, we found out that our neighbor had indeed passed away. His passing still hurts like hell. He was an amazing person and we were honored to call him friend. God bless you. I know we will see each other again someday.

###

This next loss is much more personal. One of my best friends from college passed away right before his 50th birthday. Spirit activity in our house had been extremely quiet. My son's spirit had either gone home or into hiding. I was not really sure until after this event took place. I could feel someone, a spirit in the house. It was a different feeling from my son's spirit so I ruled him out. I kept waiting for more psychic information to come into my mind or to see it. I had been feeling subtle signs of the spirit's presence for at least a day before I acknowledged it.

I remember asking my son, "Have you noticed anything or heard anything different around the house?"

He said, "In fact, I have. When I came home the last couple of nights the lid of my laptop had been shut, and I know not by me."

I told him, "I know I shut it once and Dad hasn't been in your room so the other time it shut some other way."

He was hoping it was his great uncle, who he misses fiercely, playing games with him. My gut was not so sure about that. I needed proof of it being either paranormal activity or, quite simply, bad hinges on the laptop lid. Until I had more proof, I did not say anything, either way, to my son. The feeling of this spirit hung around for a couple more days. It did not give clues at all as to who it was. I had not received a phone call from any family member so I figured it was either a previously dead relative or a friend popping by to check in. I hoped that it was a dead family member or friend spirit or a stranger who just happened to see my psychic beacon and decided to come in.

I will admit, I was happy for the return of spirit activity to the house but I was also nervous. It does mean someone has or had died. The next day I was checking in on my social network and noticed some interesting posts from a dear friend. I clicked into his site and he had reported that he was home now. He was still weak but feeling better. There was a row of posts from his other friends wishing him well, "feel better soon" and so on. Then there was another post from him. He was recovering from a stroke. It was a freak thing at his young age of 48 but everything was fine. My gut, my "psychicness" screamed out, "Tell him there is more to this! Get back to the doctor!"

I was posting that to his site while simultaneously reading a current post just under it that said, "RIP dear friend."

I went blank. My mind shut down. When I could think again, all I could think of was, Oh My God! I am too late! No...No ...No. What the hell? I was still trying to process everything and kept reading. I was hoping to get to the punchline of this sick joke. But, this was real. My college buddy had died. He was a gem among us and had been taken from us way too early. Oh my God, I was sad to the bone. We would never get to meet each other's families. Knowing that increased the pain even more. I could no longer feel my legs. I had to sit and that is when it came to me. The spirit in the house had been my buddy. I wondered if playing with my son's computer was a hint. My buddy and I both got jobs out of college with computer companies, ironically.

I never received a definitive answer from the spirit world as to whether it was him or not. Maybe I was grasping at straws because I wanted it to be him so badly. As I have thought about it over the years, I really do not need an answer from my spirits. I know in my mind and down in my soul, it was him. He was a loving father to his kids, a kind, true and giving friend… to the end. Thank you, and God bless you, buddy.

CHAPTER 11

FORETOLD EVENTS

My husband and I have been together for 28 years. The night we met, I went to my parents' house and told my mom, "I've met the man I'm going to marry!" She was surprised because I walked in and just dropped it on her like that. She had always told me I would know when I met him. She said my gut would know. We used the word gut for lack of a better one. The word "psychic" was not used except in the form of entertainment. As for my husband, he thought I was a good "guesser" and had good instincts for things. At the time, neither of us really understood what that meant.

Early in our marriage, I played pranks on my husband by using the home phone. I always knew when the phone was going to ring. Today, my conclusion is that it gives off electrical energy and I feel it. Now that we have cell phones, I do not get the same feeling even though it gives off energy. Maybe battery energy is harder for me to detect. Anyway, occasionally my husband would be by the phone when I got the feeling it was going to ring. I would ask, "Since you're by the phone, would you mind answering it?"

He would stare at me with a puzzled look on his face and then the phone would ring. His expression would then say, "You're weird!" I was almost 100% correct with the premonition of the phone ringing. He adjusted to me and started asking as he passed by the phone, "Is it going to ring? Since I'm right here, I could pick it up!"

A year and a half into wedded bliss, I got sick. That did not happen very often. I spent an entire weekend at home with the flu bug. Monday morning arrived and I was still sick. It put me in a rotten mood but I told my husband, "This should pass today and I'll be all better when you get home from work." I did make it out of bed that day but only to fall on the living room couch.

The next day, my husband handed me the phone, "Call the doctor."

I told him, "I don't need the doctor. I'll be fine in a few hours." Liar, liar, I said to myself. I admit I am the world's worst sick person. My husband did not move. He had the oddest look on his face and was just staring at me. "What?" I said.

He shook his head, "You don't know do you, Miss Gut Feelings?" I looked at him but I did not know what to say to that. He said, "You're pregnant. You need to see a doctor!"

Well, knock me over with a feather! So much for "gut feelings" when it comes to me. I found out later that same day, I was indeed pregnant. An amazing time in our lives was just beginning. Within a few days, I a had feeling come over me that I was carrying a boy. Turns out my mom knew, too. This made my husband nervous.

He said, "Your gut didn't tell you that you were pregnant.

How do you know it's a boy?" I ignored that comment

and began putting the nursery together, all in blue, of

course. He finally voiced some concern to my mom,

"What do I do?"

She told him, "Keep the receipts. It can all be

exchanged, if necessary."

Seven months had elapsed since I predicted that our

baby was a boy. It was time to find out if I was right or

not. My water broke, we piled into the car and off we

went at 2:30 a.m. to the hospital. As we drove into a

clearing at the end of our lake, this magnificent sight took

our breath away. We glanced to the left where the sky was

awash with dancing colors and light. It was the aurora

borealis. We looked at each other and my husband said,

"It's like the heavens are welcoming our son to the world!"

"Oh," I said, tearing up, "you believe me?"

He gave me the best smile a man has ever given a woman. We drove off to bring our son into this world.

A side note on this: A couple of days later, we arrived back home with boy baby in tow. In conversation with other people, we commented on the beauty of the sky that night. Not a single person we talked to had seen it... just us.

###

I dream vivid, active, full color dreams every night. Sometimes I wake up more tired than when I went to bed. I hate that. One particular dream stayed with me for days. It was a bad dream that took place in a city I did not recognize. In the dream, my husband and I were walking down a plank by a stone wall. This led us to a small, double-decked vessel, something like a tugboat. It was gray and white. The upper deck was open, with bench seating that ran all along the outer railing. While we made our way to the upper deck, the boat pulled away from its dockage. That is when it became clear that we were in the harbor of a major city. As I said, I had no idea what city this was. I looked out and noticed the water in the harbor was so very dark, midnight blue, almost black. I am seriously frightened of dark water, deep or not, but if it is dark, it is probably deep. (A girlfriend of mine is a hypnotist. She and I have discussed my fear of dark water. She thinks it could stem from a past life, a drowning, which would have obviously been traumatic.) The dream jumped ahead and the next thing I knew the ship was sinking. I yelled to my husband, "We can swim. It's not a big deal!" We were fine and simply floated around in the harbor. The dream ended.

The remnants of the dream stayed on my mind for days. My husband did not understand why it would bother me because we did not have any plans to be on the water. Days later and the dream long forgotten, we flew out on vacation. We arrived in Boston and rented a car. We drove to Maine and stayed for three days of just enjoying nature. We then drove back to Boston to spend a day and a half in the big city. I am a huge history geek so going to Boston had been something I wanted to do for many years. We thought the best thing to do was to follow the Freedom Trail. That way, we could see a great deal of the major historical sites. This turned out to be an amazing historical walking tour, which, for us, ended at the Charlestown Navy Yard. Our reason for going to the shipyard was to tour the great American treasure, the USS Constitution. It took longer than anticipated to get to the yard and then we took our sweet time touring the ship. We were now hungry and thirsty. I asked my husband, "Do you realize that Boston has the oldest tavern in American history?"

He understood the meaning of that question and started to walk me toward the exit of the yard. We did not get very far and then my husband abruptly stopped. He told me to wait where I was while he walked over to the guard shack of the ship to converse with a couple of the enlisted men. He came back over to me with a smug look. He grabbed me by the shoulders and turned me to face the opposite direction. I said, "What was that about and why did you turn me around?"

He said, "I thought, who better to ask than a couple of young enlisted guys about the location of the pub? As it turns out, this is the fastest way." Okay, not stereotyping here, but they did know exactly where the pub was located and gave us great directions. Off we went and as we walked, we stayed to the right edge of the pier.

We went down a plank, with the side of the pier now on our left, there was a stone wall. I knew that wall. I whipped my head to the right and there it was! A gray and white vessel that looked like a tugboat. I spoke out loud without realizing what I was doing, "Oh my God, it's the same ship!" I looked at my husband, and asked, "Do you remember the dream I had a couple of weeks ago about a gray and white ship?"

He looked at the ship, then back at me and said, "No shit!"

I was rattled. I'd had my first premonition dream. He remembered that in my dream the ship sank. He asked me, "Can you get on her?"

I said, "I'm fine. I really don't think she will sink."

We got on that boat and, by taking that risk, were treated to the view of a lifetime. Boston Harbor was fantastic. At the end of the ship ride and a short hike, we were at the tavern. After our beverages arrived, my husband raised his glass to mine for a toast and said, "I'm glad the only thing to get wet will be our taste buds!"

Our cousin was getting married in Massachusetts. Again, we flew to Boston, but this time we rented a car and drove south to Plymouth. We decided to tour the area. Our son, just shy of turning eight years old, had just recently studied about the Pilgrims in school so he was all for it. We pulled into town and were impressed at how lovely and quaint the town seemed to be. I had a happy feeling in my heart but I also had a strange, unsettled feeling in my brain. I have never had this feeling in my entire life. I knew, in my soul, that I had been in Plymouth, Massachusetts before that day. I had an amazing, emotional, light feeling. It was complete jubilance. It was even better than my memory of coming home from college on Christmas break (no homework, all the home cooking I could handle and presents). I have no way of proving this coming home experience was merely a "déjà vu" moment. It was, however, the happiest, heartwarming feeling I have ever known. To verify I used that word correctly, I looked up the definition of déjà vu in the dictionary. It means to have an overwhelming sense of familiarity with something or someplace that should not be familiar at all. That is EXACTLY what Plymouth, Massachusetts was for me.

###

I have visited several psychics in my life. Some were complete ripoffs and some pretty general. Some actually hit correctly on a few things and one or two have been surprisingly right on. One of those amazing psychics had been suggested by word of mouth. She did readings for groups and the price was right for the entertainment. A group of us went for it. We were at my parents' house, sitting around the living room having some wine, while the psychic got set up in the other room. She had handed each of us a plain white 3x5 card to hold. No one else was to touch it. Different? Yes, it was!

One by one, she called us into the other room for an individual reading. We would sit down and give her the card. She then proceeded to run the card over the flame of a lit candle, which put random black smudges on it. I asked, "Why do you do that?"

She said, "These smudges are what I read."

I was not believing that explanation but thought, what the hell, this is her gimmick, let her be. I figured she was concentrating on us rather than the smudges. She was picking up our electrical vibration off the card we had touched.

She looked away from the card and the candle, stared at me and said, "Okay, so who is going to read who?"

I laughed and said, "I'm not sure what you mean by that. I can't do readings."

She shrugged her shoulders and proceeded to do my reading. She told me an amazing amount of information about myself. Certainly, more than I remember now but a couple of things did stick in my mind. The events she described, and what ultimately came to be, are so crazy you will understand why I remember them so vividly. The psychic told of a friend of mine that would betray me. She thought the person might have a mental illness that was undiagnosed or simply not common knowledge. She saw the mental illness because this person, in her vision, was grainy and gray. To her, that is a sign of something being wrong or not normal. Also, because of the methodicalness this person was putting into her plan of betrayal, the psychic said, "I'm scared for you." She said she did not think it would be too much longer before this would happen. Then she said, "This person already has it all planned so be very careful." She continued, "A friend of yours will become ill and while hospitalized, she will be so ill it will distort her looks. People won't recognize her."

Then there was an event she told me about, with a smile, that I remember most. She said, "There will be an important man coming into your life. Do you understand who that might be?" I must have looked blank because she chuckled and said one word, "Husband!" I was shocked because I was not yet thinking about or looking to get married. I remember thinking, okay, I might want to pay more attention. As each day passed, I thought about what she had said. How could I not? It was a big piece of information! It did not take long for one of the above events to happen.

I woke up in the middle of the night with fierce stabbing pains in my back. On a scale of one to ten, this pain was a ten! My parents drove me to the hospital emergency room. According to the doctor, I had an infection at some point that had harbored itself and now came back to life. They admitted me right away. The next afternoon, while up for a nurse aided walk, a couple of my friends came by for a visit. They went right past me in the hall and did not recognize me!

Because of the great care and medicine, I was able to go home the next morning. Within a short time after getting out of the hospital, the person I thought was my best friend turned out to be anything but my best friend. The psychic was correct. This betrayal was totally planned and coldly methodical. It was a relief when this person was done with her game and gone. I felt safe again. Thankfully, I had help coping with this malicious event. Just before it all went down, I met a smart and wonderful man, now my husband. The bits of information the psychic gave me were very helpful. There were some tough times in those stories. It was great knowing in advance that, in the end, everything was going to be all right.

Feeling alone with my gift, I decided to associate with people I hoped would understand me. I went to my first Psychic Fair. It was interesting and you know what I mean if you have ever attended one. I say that jokingly. Actually, it was great and looking back on it, I realize it was something I knew I needed to do. I was apprehensive, of course, about attending a Psychic Fair. I talked my girlfriend into going with me. Our first impression was that is was odd, but interesting, so we stayed.

The room was the size of an elementary school gymnasium and just as loud. This huge amount of noise is bad for my senses. I get bad psychic reception like AM radio stations sound in a lightning storm. I thought some intense concentration might help clear my head so I decided to have a reading done. There were about 30 psychics sitting at tables, some were already doing readings. I was drawn to one sweet looking woman and went over to her table. She asked me to sit and took hold of my hand. We were connected, physically. She was indeed very nice but was disappointing me at first because all she hit on psychically were the typical generalities of a bad reading. I was afraid all I was going to get for the money was information I already knew. Immediately after I thought that, she opened her eyes, looked me in the face and apologized for being so general. She then hit me with two "dead on" comments. Mentally, I gave her credit for those and sincerely hoped she could keep it up.

I gave her a lot of credit for even attempting a reading in this huge, loud room. I know I could not concentrate there and she told me so. Again, right after I thought that, she looked back at me with a funny glint and said, "Wow, you are hard to read. There seems to be a lot of static. Are you feeling all right?" Still looking at me, she smiled and said, "You're really psychic. That's why I'm getting so much static. There's too much going on in here for you!"

With a sheepish look, I shook my head, yes. Well now, didn't that take care of any doubt I had about her abilities? I relaxed, she continued with my reading and said, "Your spirits and family are telling me you talk to them every day." Then she said something about being wet. I laughed out loud, apologized and explained how I pray in the shower daily to God and my spirits. She laughed, too. She said she liked that and the spirits do, too! Next she said, "Oh my gosh, besides prayer, you are very religious. I see crosses all over the place." Hmmm, interesting she would jump on that right after I told her I pray every day. I do not consider myself really religious but I do have several crosses as personal adornment. I had recently received a cross on a chain from my uncle. He gave it to me just before he passed away. It was my aunt's and she had preceded him in death. This was not connecting to him for me. I wanted it to. I needed more and hoped she had it. She continued but on a new subject, "You're packed and ready to move, not physically, but in your mind." She continued, "Like letting go of a job and moving into a new career." That was right on! I did not want to work in our school district any longer. I wanted to write.

She then moved on to my spirit line up. There are spirits that you talk to and think about all the time. They could also be spirits that chose to stay close to you because of their love for you. I was bored by this until she gave details about them. "First," she said, "I'm picking up on a strong woman who gave you great counsel during her lifetime, about you, your family and your place in life." "Second," she continued, "okay, another strong woman, she had thick glasses and told me to tell you she is the one that had great parties for the family at her house."

I did not tell the psychic, but the first woman was my grandmother on my dad's side of the family and the second was my grandmother on my mom's side. The clues and details she gave were right on so I knew exactly who she was talking about. She gave me enough correct, unique details that I knew there was not a chance in hell she was just guessing. My dad's mom and I would talk for hours about everything. She helped me through an emotionally hard childhood. I knew, felt, and made observations about people more than any small child should. The grandmother on my mom's side did have very thick eyeglasses but that could be common at her age. However, the other details about her were very telling. She hosted wonderful family reunions. All of the families came to their farm. She is the grandma who taught me to bake.

The psychic then asked, "Who is the priest?"

I said, "I have no idea, maybe it's someone on my husband's side of the family."

She didn't think so but moved on. "Tell me, who is the person with Alzheimer's Disease or the person who listens but cannot talk?" I didn't have time to answer. She went on, "This spirit says you will know. I see crosses again." I had a feeling it was my uncle that just passed away. He was in a coma of sorts at the end of his life. My uncle's wish was to pass away at home. My wonderful cousins made sure his every wish was fulfilled. When I finally saw him, it was as though he was just sleeping. I desperately wanted him to wake up. I told him I was sorry that I did not get there sooner and that I loved him very much. He passed away the next night. The psychic said, "He's saying he could hear all the people who came to see him and to tell them he could. You will know who to tell." She said she saw crosses again. That was it. She had run over her time. She said, "That was fun and easy once we cleared the static!" I thanked her and we left.

The matter of the crosses and the man in the coma kept my mind going the entire ride home. I walked into a peaceful, empty house, poured a glass of wine and went out on to the deck to think and get some fresh air. My neighbor was working in her yard and we started to talk.

Her husband had recently died so the conversation quickly moved to that. It was at this point she told me her husband had intended to be a priest and was actually in the seminary at one point. I would not doubt my mouth was hanging open when she said that. Was this the priest reference the psychic was talking about? I knew he was not able to communicate before he passed away. He, too, was in a coma of sorts.

Do I say something about what I was told? I did not know what to do but thought, why else would our conversation land on the discussion of his desire to be a priest? We have lived next door to each other for over 25 years and I was just hearing this for the first time. I do not believe there is such a thing as a coincidence so I told her what the psychic had said. I had delivered the message. She got tears in her eyes and thanked me for telling her. I also told my cousins and my mom because it may have been my uncle. I covered all bases. Everyone appreciated the comforting feeling it gave them. I think that was all right. I did not, and still do not, see anything wrong with giving comfort to grieving, emotionally hurting friends and family. Besides, what they choose to do with the information is up to them. It could be they were simply being kind, hearing me out, and then they just let it go at that.

CHAPTER 12

OUR OLD SOUL

When our son was three years old, he said something to me that I will never forget. The two of us were working away in the kitchen. I was making dinner at the counter and he was on the floor building a castle using plastic food storage containers from the cupboard. While working away at my feet, he looked up at me and said, "Mama, can I tell you sompen'?"

I looked down at him and said, "Of course, you can tell me anything."

He said, "You know this is my last time here."

I turned and crouched down in front of him. We looked each other directly in the eyes, without talking. I peered as deep as I could into his beautiful, dark brown eyes. I realized just how deep and intelligent this little person was. I had no doubt he knew what he was talking about. This was not just a random statement. Goosebumps rose up on my entire body. Even the hair on my head was standing on end.

I knew in my heart what he was going to say next but I played a bit silly and asked, "What do you mean, not back into the kitchen?"

In his own bright and unique little style, he said, "No silly, here on Earth! This is my last time because I'm a very old soul."

I abruptly sat down on the floor as my mind tried to register what he had just said. I admit, I did not expect that high level of an answer. Even if I did, he was only three years old. Still face to face, I gently took his little hands in mine and said, "Yes, you are an old soul, aren't you?"

He stood, stepped over my legs, wrapped his little arms around my neck in a sweet hug and said very casually, "I knew you would understand."

I hugged him back for all I was worth while tears were streaming down my face. I said, "Who else but another old soul would?"

He pulled back to look me in the face and we laughed. I took his laugh as one of relief that I actually understood. He was glad someone else now knew his truth. Mine, of course, was a laugh of "HOLY CRAP!" Now I knew, but I did not know what to do with that information. I had a feeling our lives were never going to be the same. (It has been one hell of an interesting ride, for sure!) He let go and plopped back down on the floor to finish his soon to be amazing storage container castle.

Just as this castle creation was finished, he asked me to look at it and casually added, "You know, Mama, I'm not sure how I know this, I just do." This line of conversation was shocking but I did not question it. I, too, thought he was an old soul. I needed to hold him again so I reached down and swung him up into my arms. We hugged until he wanted down.

Having the responsibility of our child both scared and amazed me. I was also flattered that he would choose to spend his last lifetime with us. You see, I believe that we choose the parents to be born to so we will learn from those best suited to expose or teach us in this lifetime what it is we have not learned yet in other lifetimes. I was flattered but maybe we are so screwed up that we were his best choice to assure he would learn what he needed to.

I told my husband and my mom about my conversation with him and said to them both, "I think I'm too screwed up to do a proper job of raising him." I really believed that at the time.

My mom said, "You and Steve are perfect. He chose you two."

I agree now but, at the time, I simply needed some reassurance. Many years have passed since this event, not all great, but certainly not all bad. The tough times that we have had, which thank you God have not been many, we refer to as speed bumps in life. Simply bumps that come and go.

The very next week, I was still digesting the old soul conversation when my son casually mentioned to me that there was a man in his room at night. Talk about a statement that ignites every single one of your parental senses! This raised all the warning flags at once. He said, "It's a bit scary, but all he does is stand in the corner and stare out the window."

I asked him, "That's all he ever does?"

"Yes," was all he said.

I knew there was not an actual man coming into my son's room at night. From my own psychic abilities and past experiences, I had a feeling he was seeing a spirit. Like mother, like son. I wanted more information. How long does he stand there? What did he look like? What was he wearing? I also did not want to ask too many questions and scare my son. I thought perhaps this was a harmless residual haunt. That is when the energy is there but the spirit is not. It is a mark in time that repeats over and over. I found this extremely interesting, never having seen one before, so I limited my questions.

Over a snack of animal crackers I asked, "What does the man by the window look like?"

He said, "Solid, but not really, oh and all black."

"Does he have a face or clothing?"

He said, "No."

That was that. He was done talking about this subject so I dropped it for a couple of days. The spirit really did not worry me as long as it didn't bother my son. Besides, a residual haunt will happen and we cannot stop it. A few days had passed and my son again brought up the topic of this spirit person in his room. He said, "He's back!"

I asked, "Is he a full guy, like with legs and feet?"

He said, "I'm not sure about feet because the end of my bed is in the way."

Again, the conversation was dropped. It was not an easy thing for me to let happen, but I did. I thought if I made a big deal of it he might get scared. I told my husband, "Since he is seeing spirits at three years old, this is probably going to be a part of his life, for the rest of his life. He will need us to help him through it all." Everything was nice, quiet and routine for the next month. The quiet ended the morning our son got up and told me that the man had moved.

He said, "I woke in the night and the man was bent over me while I was lying in bed. He was looking right into my face! I pulled the covers up over my head and woke up just now."

Maybe this was not just a residual haunt. I told my son, "Next time call me and I will come to your room." I wish I had thought to let him know he can tell the spirit to go away. We ended the conversation and it was time to feed that little tummy. Cereal became the new topic. While he ate, I again brought up the subject of his spirit.

I asked him, "Do you want the spirit removed from the house? For him to go away?"

He said, "Why mom? He isn't hurting anything. He's just watching."

The old soul has spoken. After a short time, we figured out the spirit is the man from whom we had purchased the house. Stephen's bedroom had been this man's office or possibly the den. He had been ill when he sold us the house and was moving to Arizona due to his doctor's advice. They were hoping the dry desert air would help. We wished him well. He was a very nice man.

My husband and I were discussing our son's bedroom spirit. I felt it odd that I had not realized he was around and wondered how long he had been in our house. We do not know when this man passed away. We surmised that his heavy smoking habit took him too soon. He easily could have been here in our house for years before we realized it. I think, too, we didn't realize it because he was here for our son, not for us. The entrance to our son's room is now off the hall. Before we gutted his room, we had to go through the furnace room to get in there. That was not suitable for our needs. We replaced everything. The floor, walls, and ceiling… everything. Remodeling is something that can stir up spirit activity. Spirits often think it is still their house and want to know what the hell you are doing to it! We have had a few guests stay in that room over the years. No one has ever said anything out of the ordinary happened.

There is a spirit, that is a true residual haunt, in the area of my son's room. As I mentioned earlier, this paranormal activity is energy only. It is like playing a movie over and over. It is a snapshot in time that keeps repeating. This residual, male spirit comes out of the wall between my son's bedroom door and the furnace room door. The furnace room was not always used for that purpose. It is one of the original rooms of the old cottage and it was the kitchen at one point in time. After the spirit comes of out the wall, he travels straight across the small vestibule, goes out the sidewall of the house and then out into our side yard. The spirit never diverges from his set pattern. He never looks around or registers his surroundings. It is the same thing over and over, two to three times a day on average. He has shown up as many as a dozen times in one day. When I see him float past, not walk, he appears to only be about 5 feet tall and he fades away just below the knee. I never saw this spirit until after our son's spirit arrived. I am not sure why or if they are connected in some way. The day I sat down to start this book, he went back and forth so many times it made me dizzy. The energy in the entire house was at the highest level I have ever felt. I hope that means the spirits were excited for me to begin this journey.

The spirit that hangs out in my son's room has chosen to appear for me several times. A couple of times, he appeared while I was trying to sleep and other times in different parts of the house. Those places are what the following stories are about.

My son had an opportunity to go to Germany with his high school, foreign language class for three weeks during the summer. He had been gone almost a week. I was adjusting to the idea of his absence but awoke one night out of a sound sleep. Confused as to the reason, I blamed my bladder and got up to use the bathroom. The bathroom is across the hall. Just as I was going to step over the threshold of the bathroom, out of habit, I looked left toward my son's room. I stopped and backed up one step. I had to verify that what I just saw was actually what I thought I saw. Down the hall, in front of my son's door, was the opaque, black shape of a man. His feet were spread apart and his hands planted on his hips. In this stance, he looked pissed off. His questions popped into my mind in a flash. His stance and projection told the whole story. He wanted to know where his boy was. It was really quite humorous, but not in the middle of the night. I just wanted to go back to bed. I did, now, need to use bathroom so I answered him with a hot temper. "My son is not home. He is in Germany and you know you should go home, to Heaven!" With that, I tended to business and went back to bed. The spirit was not there on my way back to bed. I had a bit of remorse about being so crabby to him but thought I would talk to the spirit tomorrow and apologize. As I was quietly getting back into bed my husband said, "Did we have company?"

I said, "Yes, we did and he was a bit put out that his boy isn't home and in bed. He was demanding an answer! I take it you heard what I told him. I'm not sure how that will go over."

My husband asked, "Will that work?"

I told him, "I'll let you know!" As it turns out, the spirit did not go home to Heaven. He just stayed away until our son returned from his trip.

We walked in the back door after picking our son up at the airport. I said, "Drop the suitcases here in the laundry room. No reason to have to bring it all back. We'll load the washing machine right now to get things going." My son and I stood there in the laundry room. We both turned and looked down the hall toward the living room. There he was, my son's spirit, in broad daylight, looking back down the hall at us. I said to my son, "The welcoming committee is here!" Once noticed, the spirit slowly, yet dramatically, faded away. My son told my husband and me the spirit appeared later in his bedroom to see if he was in bed. Still being on European time, our son was wide awake and caught his visitor.

These events truly rate as some of the best paranormal experiences of my life. A full body apparition, with or without attitude, is a remarkable sight to behold.

At one point, I really thought that we should at least attempt to send my son's spirit home. This caused me much distress. I had mixed emotions. I would miss him but had always thought that, if possible, Heaven was where a spirit belonged. Isn't God looking for him? Weren't family members and friends looking for him? I assumed yes to all those questions.

Approximately a year later, my son was now away at college. My husband and I were home with a lonely spirit on our hands. In a previous chapter, I talked about being pestered by our son's spirit at this time. Because of that, I decided to try and send him home. I thought I should wait until our son came home for a weekend visit and talk this over with him. If he agreed, we would say goodbye and send him on his way. We decided that the spirit, even though seemingly very comfortable here, might be stuck and not know how to move on.

Our son was not sure about this and said, "This feels like we're forcing him into a place he would go on his own, if he really wanted to go." He continued, "Like old people, when their kids move them into a nursing home, for their own good!"

I thought, "Ouch," and said, "Let's talk to him and see what feeling we get from him. We will do his bidding." We chuckled then I said out loud to the spirit, "We think you need to go home. We think that you have family and friends that are waiting for you. We think Heaven is where you belong. Yes, I do think you will go to Heaven, in case that was a question. We do not think there is anything to fear in crossing over. It seems it should be a peaceful thing to do. Do you agree? It's all right to move on. Your boy will be fine. He's growing up into his own life."

I am saying this, while wondering if the spirit is thinking, "How in the hell does she know?" I told my husband about it all when he got home from work later that evening.

He said, "Did you give it your best try or not?"

I asked, "What does that mean?"

He laughed and said, "Because you don't really want him to go. You're doing it out of what you think is right and should be done, correct?"

He was right on both counts. He knows me so well. The house was entirely too quiet when our son went back at school. My husband was at work and the spirit was nowhere to be seen or heard. I missed his noises and presence as much as I thought I would. I was still not convinced he was gone but I went about my daily life.

Within a week, I complained to my husband, "The house is creepy. It's too quiet." He laughed. I continued, "There are no shadows moving on the walls, no odd movements in my peripheral vision (except for the residual guy), no footstep sounds in the hall, no creaking and popping of thresholds. Even the dog is bored by the calm. I think she misses the activity, too, it entertained her like television does us." With that, I stopped whining and we went about our evening. I knew I would get over this empty feeling. After all, I had done a good deed sending the spirit home, right? I am left with great memories and stories of him. I hope he is having fun in Heaven. There is a part of me that hopes he is merely mad at me and staying away, but it has been weeks. He would have to be really stubborn to hide this long. I miss him like a missing family member. Silly, I know.

Midweek, there was a ghost hunting show on television that I always watched. This particular week, they happened to talk about having feelings of sadness after you help someone cross over. I cracked up because they called that normal. Our son came home for the weekend that Friday. His spirit reappeared in his bedroom. He had been waiting for his boy to come home. That made me feel better.

CHAPTER 13

CONFUSED, SCARED AND CURRENT

HAPPENINGS

This chapter is dedicated to events that happened over the past 40 year period. They have confused me, scared me, and/or struck me as odd. I am also including some spiritual events that have taken place around me while I have been working on this book.

###

Spiritual events are something I do not take with a grain of salt or at face value. I look at and question everything about every event. What I look and hope for is that an event will repeat itself or a spirit will reappear. The reoccurrence is sometimes that same day, two days later or maybe a week later. As long as it is the same activity or the same spirit, I give the event credence and define it as spiritual activity. Then, as far as I am concerned, it is not just a noise from an unseen place or an apparition due to eye strain. Since I am the only one that has seen or heard a good deal of the events I have been talking about, I love it when I have confirmation from one of my family members, even if only the dog. Confirmation lets me know I am not crazy or at least not crazy alone. I would not include something in this book if I did not absolutely believe it happened. I do believe all of the events in this book to be real and of a spiritual nature. My gift is growing and ever changing. I am learning more almost every day about the spirit world and about myself.

###

The next event occurred in the middle of fall in Michigan. It was 48 degrees out and raining, not lovely. I could not get the house warm and thought cooking in the oven would do the trick. So, I baked a chicken. While standing at the kitchen sink that day and cleaning this massive, whole bird, I thought about my grandma (Gma, is how I wrote it in letters to her). I remembered how she used to fuss over cleaning poultry, especially the huge turkey at Thanksgiving. When I was growing up, she would come the day before the holiday and thoroughly clean the turkey. She would be stationed at the sink with that task. My mom and I would be buzzing around her in the kitchen doing other dinner tasks. We were totally entertained with her ongoing commentary on the condition of the bird. My grandparents had a farm so she knew about the condition of a bird. Her comments were mostly about the pinfeathers. On a turkey, they can be huge. She would pick and talk. It was great. I deeply miss all of that. There were some tiny condition issues on my chicken and I said out loud to her, "Gma, you would think I picked a lousy bird. It needs lots of cleaning!" I laughed about that and then, WHAM! There was a huge, loud slamming sound from some place in the house. It was such a big and loud noise that it filled the house which made it impossible to pinpoint where it came from. I immediately washed my hands and proceeded to look around the entire house for something that had fallen off a shelf and crashed onto the floor. I went room by room but there was nothing out of place. I even went outside to check the yard, our roof, and the neighbor's houses. I also looked to see if there was a car crash out front but everything looked fine. I had never heard this noise before and it scared the hell out of me. Later, I told my son what had happened. He said, "Gma must have thought the pin feather story was pretty funny!"

###

This is a case of knowing you are not alone in a room. Many times over the years I have woken up from a nap and caught a glimpse of someone across the room, usually seated in a chair. After researching and consulting people in the psychic field, everything pointed to the same answer, it is my spirit guide. I was told that a spirit guide would come to be with you, to watch over you and make sure you are safe at times when you are vulnerable. While I was asking the psychics about those events, I also asked about another. I questioned if a family member might just as easily come watch over you or is it only spirit guides. I was referring to the time I had a nasty head cold and sought the comfort of my bed. I was sleeping like a rock but hours later I was awakened in the middle of the night. I was being held in someone arms. Honest to God, I felt someone holding me. I could see and feel someone's arms cradle me like a baby. I looked up into a face and an outline of a head and shoulders, but the facial features stayed in shadow. It was an amazing feeling. I was completely safe, comfortable and had someone nursing me back to health. I know it sounds unbelievable. I believe it for the simple facts that I both saw and felt someone there. It would never have crossed my mind to dream up a nursemaid. I woke the next day feeling well enough to go to work.

Have you ever thought of a song, talked about a song or had a meaningful song weirdly play for you at an appropriately precise time? It has happened to me several times but the time I am referring to now relates particularly to my writing. This song has to be at least five years old now. In its day, it played excessively but now only seems to play when I get off task or question what I am doing with this book.

Years ago, I was working on a different writing project and had asked my spirit guides for guidance. Right after I asked for help, the song I am talking about played on the radio. It struck me as odd. Why did they keep playing a song for me whose lyrics were telling me "the rest is still unwritten?" I paid no more attention to it because the song was correct. The book was not yet finished. This same thing happened several more times. I would question if I should continue writing my book and then that song would play for me. I did end up putting that book aside and started a fiction version of a paranormal novel.

I could not get the idea of writing a fiction novel out of my head so I thought, why not? With that decision made, I got into my car to do some errands and the same song came on the radio. I arrived at my first destination and I walked into a store. The first thing that hit me was the song that was playing in the store, that same song. Maybe that was not so odd, but truly what was odd was that it was playing from the same spot it was when I got out of my car. It could not be the same station because it wouldn't be playing from the same spot in the song.

Approximately 40 minutes later, I checked out at the store, went out to my car, started the engine, the radio came on, and that song was playing, AGAIN. Moreover, it was playing from the same spot in the song, AGAIN. This was the same radio station as before. I had not changed it. My spirits must think I am thicker than wood. I was finally paying attention.

When I got home, I started this book, a nonfiction version of my paranormal life and that song has not played for me since. I have to add here, when I sat down and physically started to write these words down on paper, the energy level in the house sharply increased. I heard thumping and bumping sounds coming from down the hall. A good sign? One can only hope.

###

The spirit activity in the house increased considerably over several months this last winter. Enough so that I checked with my son to see what activity he had experienced over that time. I also wanted to double check that he and his friends had not been dabbling in anything occult or playing with a Ouija board. I do not like them. I think they open portals. These are doors into the spirit world that let in anything that is there, good or bad. My son said, "No, of course not, I know better than that." The activity continued and that was okay. It was not activity of a bad nature. For instance, I was talking to my son in the living room when, from behind him, a blurred head and face zoomed up close. It was fast but I noticed there were shoulders and part of a torso. The rest of the body faded away below the hips. He looked young, maybe early 20's, with short, light brown hair. He had a pleasantness about him. It was not spooky. Honestly, it was odd, startling and fun. I got the feeling he was merely an inquisitive spirit and he was checking us out and our conversation. My son said, "Now what?" I laughed and told him about the spirit guy.

This next event occurred immediately after the last one. It was creepy, though. Because of this second event, I still questioned whether someone had used a Ouija board. It does not have to happen in your own home. It could have been at a neighbor's house and the spirits were attracted to us.

I was seated in the bathroom and no one else was home. I left the door open. My attention was drawn into the hall. A short figure appeared. It was about three to four feet tall with a skim milk, grayish colored body. It looked as if it was wearing a bad toupee full of dark orange hair. It was standing there with its back to me when it very slowly and deliberately turned just its head almost half way around. He turned slowly and looked me right in the face. The damn thing's skin was so pasty white it was translucent and with no facial features whatsoever. Then, it just faded away. Odd? Hell yes! It had my attention. Talk about a captive audience! I do not allow creepy spirits into my house and said so very vocally.

Later I checked with my son and he had never seen anything like him. He is happy to keep it that way. As soon as I could, I checked with my girlfriend. She had just moved and left a spirit at her old house. I asked her what he had looked like. I thought maybe he was lonely and came for a visit. The spirit she described, including baseball attire, was nothing like what I had seen.

Consequently, the little creeper is still a mystery. I did sternly tell it that it was not welcome here and demanded he leave and stay away. My house, my rules. For extra security, I said a prayer and included, "No evil comes from us, so no evil comes to us." I am happy to report this creepy spirit has not been seen since. Thank you, God.

###

I recently spotted a spirit but not in my own home. This fits into this chapter because I have never had the honor of this happening before. This event took place at a friend's home. Every few months, a group of us moms get together. Our sons were all on the high school swim team together. We alternate homes, bring a dish to pass, a bottle of wine and listening ears. This particular night, during one of the many conversations, the woman who owns the house got up to get a book off a shelf. Behind her was a wide open area and just beyond that was the dining room. She grabbed the book and was standing in the opening to the other room when, just behind her, I

spotted something starting to take shape. It became a full

bodied apparition. It was skinny, tall, had slate gray

coloring, wore a shirt and denim colored pants. Best of

all, it was dancing. He was doing a mix between old

dance styles called The Monkey and The Funky Chicken.

He basically had his arms swinging in front of him from

head to knees, alternating his arms. I said to myself,

"Check out the spirit playing around over there. He's

dancing!" When that thought popped into my head, the

spirit who had not been paying us any attention, froze in

the middle of his awesome moves, turned his head and

looked me directly in the eyes. I was looking back at him

in the eyes with a huge "cat ate the canary" grin on my

face. I could tell by the shocked look on his face I had

surprised him and he took off. He left so fast. His

movements blurred as if a vacuum had sucked him away.

Shortly after this event, I needed to use the bathroom

there at my friend's house. The bathroom was around the

corner, where I assumed the dancing man had taken off to hide. I could feel him and knew he was peeking at me through the railing from the top of the stairs. But, I let him be. I think I had shaken him up enough for one night. He was not there to hurt my friend. He seemed to be a fun loving clown. I did not tell her that I had seen him. She is content with her beliefs and it might only have served to freak her out. Tempting, yes, but maybe cruel. So, I left well enough alone and kept it to myself.

###

This event goes back to when I was getting married. A delightfully exciting time but it was also a bit sad for me. It was exciting because I was marrying a wonderful man. However, it was sad thinking of all the loving family members that had passed away and would not be attending (especially Grandma Bruce). I remember saying so out loud and admitting I had to let it go.

I do not remember what length of time went by after saying that I wished my grandmother would be there with me when a package arrived at my door. A delivery service coming to the house with wedding gifts was the daily norm but only from invited guests. Today, unbeknownst to us, we received a gift from a person not on our guest list. I opened the cardboard shipping box and revealed a bright red box with a card on top. I did as I was taught and opened the card first. I read the card and had to sit down. I was shaking from head to toe. The gift was from a close girlfriend of Grandma Bruce's. Lord, this woman had to be over 90 years old, and furthermore, how did she even knew I was getting married? The card said that she would not miss giving a wedding gift to Myrtle's beloved granddaughter. I was blown away! I assumed all of my grandmother's friends had passed away. Grandma had been gone for 17 years. It was a miraculous event, gift and day. Immediately, I called my parents on the phone. They were also shocked beyond words. They were equally touched as I was at her thoughtfulness. What a testament to my grandma. This woman thought that much of her to do this, after so many years. I sent her a card and thanked her for the beautiful gift of a Waterford crystal bell. I made sure she understood that this told me my beloved grandma was indeed going to be at my wedding. xo

###

I had a feeling something was about to happen. I did not know what, when or to whom. I had a suspended feeling, a very strong one. I concentrated on the feeling and tried to pull in details. I had not ever done this so I did not know exactly how. What I tried did not work so I chose to ignore the bombardment of feelings aimed at me and get ready for our family vacation. We had planned a family trip to Chicago, just the three of us, for a long weekend of big city adventures. On the way there, I said something to my husband about being unsettled, that something bad was coming. He understood and made sure we kept our cell phone close by at all times. We did not want to worry our son so we did not say anything to him. However, I think he knew something was up.

After two fun filled days, our hotel room phone rang early and woke us up to some bad news. I had succeeded pushing aside my anxiety because the cell phone had been left in the car all night after having driven to dinner. The call was from my sister-in-law. She told us to come home because my mom had gone into the hospital. A part of her lower intestine had ruptured and she was in rough shape. Her blood thinner medicine was postponing the doctors from operating. It was a waiting game on the blood thinner. They could not operate until her levels had dropped enough. I raced to be there before she went in to surgery. We got to my mom's bedside as they were preparing to wheel her off to the operating room. I won my race and had a moment to tell her, "I love you, be strong." Now I prayed she would win her battle.

Many hours later she came out of surgery and went right into the ICU. They had her on a ventilator. I was scared to death she would never be strong enough to come off that machine. I sat by her bed, hour after hour. I had a lot of time to think and what I thought of was God and Mother God. I had read, years earlier, about Mother God and how she is in charge of miracles, health and healing. I prayed right then and there! I asked her to please help my mom. Every morning, as always, I prayed in the shower but now I added prayers to Mother God. I asked her to help my mom each day with something different, whatever it was that my mom needed toward the next step of her recovery.

I would do what was needed at home and then head over to the hospital. For ten straight days, I would walk in to my mom's room and either the event I had asked Mother God to help make happen was in process or it would have already happened. These days were truly a miracle, especially since I was not even sure I believed in Mother God. I properly thanked Mother God every day and on the tenth day, I watched my parents pull away from the hospital in their car. My mom was waving and smiling at me from the front seat.

Occasionally, my experiences come in waves, one right after another, or grouped together with a couple of events per day, over several days.

My girlfriend and I headed off for a weekend in the central part of lower Michigan to visit a mutual friend from high school. We stayed in a cozy "mom and pop" motel just outside of the town where she lives. After a fun filled day, we got back late to our motel room ready to get some sleep. It had been a long day. The room was classically set up, two double beds with a night stand in between. There was a television at the foot of the beds. We put on our pajamas, washed our faces and were lying on our beds talking about the day. She rolled over, faced away from me and fell asleep. I grabbed the remote control from the nightstand and aimed it at the television. I spotted a little girl standing at the foot of my friend's bed. The little girl had long, brown hair to her waist and a light colored (possibly yellow), short sleeve babydoll dress. She was just standing there, staring straight ahead toward the wall and the headboard of the other bed. It did not seem like she was seeing what was currently in our room. I noticed how blank the look on her face was and wondered if she was a residual haunt, a sweet snapshot in time.

Finally, I turned the television off. She was still standing there, staring straight ahead. I was tired and went to sleep. I am not sure how long she stayed. I did wonder, before I slept, who she was and if she had died by drowning in the lake just outside our room. I woke up the next morning and looked to that same area in the room. She was gone, just as I thought she would be. I decided to wait to tell my friend until she was more awake, showered and had that all important coffee.

Just as we were ready to head out the door in search of breakfast, the oddest thing happened. Something flew between us. We figured it was a big bug like a moth but could not tell because it moved too fast. It was October, in mid Michigan so it was chilly and the bugs were pretty scarce. It was so big, I asked, "Did you hear any noise coming from it, buzzing or flapping from its wings?"

She said, "No, and we should have because it came so close and it was huge."

We agreed, that was weird. Without speaking a word to each other, we started to search the room. We had to make sure the room was "all clear" before we had breakfast. The room was not that big so it should have been easy to find. She took half the room and I the other half. We checked the entire room, twice, and still did not find anything. My girlfriend looked at me and said, "Okay, I want the story. That wasn't a bug was it?"

I told her, "I'm not absolutely positive it was a bug. I think it might have been the spirit of a little girl I saw at the foot of your bed last night."

I needed caffeine and had a dull headache. It was now made worse by my girlfriend yelling, "WHAT?" I ushered her by the arm out into the car. I told her everything about the little girl during our drive to breakfast. I included the fact that she was harmless. Many hours later, now after midnight, we came back to the room, did another bug check and got into bed. The little girl did not appear again. It was about the same time as the night before so maybe it was not a residual haunt. I never told my girlfriend that part.

Spiritual activity at my home had been wildly busy the week before this trip so the little girl spirit fit right into my week. When we returned from our trip, my son filled me in on all the spiritual activity he'd had happen day and night while I was away. I do not draw a connection to my son's spirit filled weekend and our motel visitor. I simply think it was two sensitives having simultaneous experiences, hundreds of miles apart.

CHAPTER 14

SPIRITS, SPIRITS, SPIRITS

This is not a chapter I had planned on writing but the spirits seemed to have another idea about that. This chapter is about those events that began as soon as the first word was written down on paper for this book. They have continued happening every time I sit and write. I started this book with a bit of trepidation. Honestly, I was afraid that if I put my experiences on paper for all to see, my gift might disappear. I am happy to report that my gifts are still intact! In fact, they have become stronger. One thing that has changed is that my son's spirit, for me, has gone away. My son has not seen him for a while but he can feel him.

When I finally sat down to write the words that I was being told were unwritten, the house went crazy with energy and noise. The energy in the house was that of a party, happy and light. I was surrounded by it. I could not tell you where the energy and noise were radiating from because it was everywhere. It was quite an experience and buzz!

The day before I started writing, I felt a spirit was lurking around in the house but I did not have time to deal with it. The next day, I sat and tried to pull the spirit closer. I wanted to communicate, but to no avail, so I went on with my day and my writing. It was becoming irritating. I could feel the spirit come closer then back off. I felt unsettled and could not concentrate. I tried one more time to talk to it, "Who are you and can I help you in anyway?" There was no answer or sign but I did feel it pulling further away. I said, "Fine, be that way!" and went to take a shower. It was date night with my husband.

As always, I was saying my prayers in the shower. I turned quickly to my left to grab the shampoo. HOLY COW! There in the shower behind me was a huge face with a big grin on its lips. Oh, I was mad as hell and sternly told the male spirit, "Get the hell out of my shower and stay out." He was out and apparently staying out but I kept mumbling about how he had invaded my private sanctuary. How dare he?

There was a slight knock at the bathroom door. My husband poked his head in and asked, "Are you all right?"

I didn't even have to look, I could hear the smile in his voice. "Yes, I'm fine, just mad."

I was laughing but, honestly, severely displeased and shocked to find a spirit in the shower with me. I realized at this point that spirits have no boundaries. This spirit was a "Peeping Tom." I knew I had to learn how to set boundaries for them. I send out a verbal order, "This incident will not repeat itself." I have not, and do not,

expect to find any more spirits in the shower with me.
Let me put it this way, "I better not!"

I do my writing in different locations around the house. Sometimes I write at the dining room table or I will use a tray and sit on the couch. With good fortune, I can be out on the deck in good weather. This particular day, I was working while seated on the couch. I had my laptop in front of me on the ottoman, really lost in what I was typing. All of a sudden, I felt creeped out. I looked up from my work and saw a spirit person down the hall, toward the back door. My eyes were tired from writing and typing. I thought possibly I was seeing things and then I heard a noise that matched his movement. It happened quickly so I do not know what the spirit looked like. It seemed to be a streak across the laundry room doorway and, if not for the corresponding noise, I would have thought it was just my tired eyes. This was too fast for the residual spirit. He casually floats across the hall. I do think it was a man. I got a fast psychic picture in my mind of a male, but that is all.

This event happened after I started the book but it is not related to my writing. Our whole family had a long weekend of graduation parties so we were not home much. If we were, it was not for any great length of time. By Sunday night, we were exhausted and stuffed with party food. We crawled into bed about 10 p.m. but both my husband and I tossed and turned. We hoped sleep would come soon. It was about 10:30 p.m. when both of us were just about asleep when I heard a noise in the back of the house. It was nothing big, just loud enough, and out of place enough, to wake me up. It was not a noise our house usually makes so I thought it deserved attention. I laid there for a few minutes. There were no more noises of that type, or any other, so I could relax. When I was just about to fall asleep again, I heard another noise in roughly the same area in the back of the house.

This time it woke up my husband. I was surprised he did not wake up before because he hears everything. He actually didn't wake up from the noise, rather, he woke up because I was awake. He asked, "What's up?"

I said, "I just heard a noise in the back of the house, second one actually in that area. It was out of place."

He said, "Well, if it were an intruder, Lola would have been off the bed like a rocket so don't worry."

He was right but I got up anyway. I was awake so I might as well use the bathroom. I was about to step into the hall and the back door blasted open. My son walked in and he frightened me. I asked him, "How long have you been around the house, like in the garage?"

He said, "Just getting home."

Okay, so it was not him. The noise had come from inside the house. I glanced around and nothing seemed out of place. I decided they were just phantom sounds so I went back to bed.

When I got into bed, I laid down on my right side. I hoped to get Lola to cuddle up with me so I would relax and fall right to sleep. Usually, all I have to do is pat the bed, call her name and she comes right over. Not this time. She would not acknowledge me and stranger yet, she would not take her eyes off the right side of the foot of the bed. I tried several more times to get her attention but she would not avert her stare. I kept looking in the area that she was staring but I did not see anything. I did not even sense anything. She continued to stare at the same spot for several more minutes. Her head started slowly turning to the left as if she were following a moving object. I kept trying to see or sense what she was looking at, all the while wondering why I could not see it. Her head and gaze kept turning to the left and then came to a stop. She was looking directly behind me. It was creepy. I stayed calm, turned my head, and glanced back over my hip, still nothing appeared. I knew there had to be something there. Otherwise, Lola's attention would never have stayed that attuned for that length of time. I glanced back at Lola and then back over my hip. I whispered in a stern voice to the unseen thing, "Go away." Immediately, I looked back to Lola. She blinked and laid her head down on the blanket with a sigh. I knew then that whatever had held her attention was no longer there.

Sleep did not find me for a while. I kept trying to put this together. The dog was not scared or mad. She did not growl but was mesmerized with whatever it was. Why couldn't I see it or feel it? How did it elude my gift that way? I believe the noises down the hall and this new event were connected. I am not sure who or what it was or what the purpose of the visit was.

I had a spiritual visitor in the house again yesterday. It had me wondering about the spirit that used to be in my son's room. I asked out loud, "Are you hiding or did you go home?" I said this as I walked in the hall to put something in the pantry. I turned around to head to the laundry room and there he was for a split second, just outside my son's room. He made me a happy woman. I thanked him for visiting and letting me see him.

CHAPTER 15

FINDING PEACE

Now you know my story. All the secrets, the bottled up senses, the hurt feelings, the lies, and the fright I have kept private for over 40 years. The fright I am talking about was not just of the things I could see and hear, it was also of the ones I could not but suspected were there. Even more frightful than that was the "what if?" What if someone found out about my psychic abilities? Would I be labeled crazy, or worse, institutionalized? My goal was to be "normal" like everyone else. I worked hard at blending in but in the end, hiding was easier.

So then, the question, why tell people now? Why let out all my secrets? It is simple. I have come to an age when I can accept and embrace all of my gifts. I appreciate the journey and the woman the spirits have helped me become. It helps, too, that at this point in my life I do not concern myself with what others think of me.

I must also mention society when answering this "why now" question. People of today are more accepting of gifted people, those with a sixth sense. Year after year, I have witnessed improvements in attitudes about these topics. Because of the focus on this topic on cable television (and in some other forms of publication), people are regularly exposed to information regarding hauntings, spirits, angels and psychics. My finding is that people feel freer to discuss what they saw on television or read that might have mirrored an event in their personal lives.

An example of this is the conversation I personally overheard while sitting in a coffee shop. While discussing a paranormal event, one woman said to another, "Amazing they would show that on TV. It happened just that way to me several years back!" By the look on her face, the woman hearing the story did not think her friend had just lost her mind. I was shocked and pleased by the lack of a negative reaction. As a whole, this is why I talk about all of this now. That, and I think many people believe they should learn more about the subject because they are having experiences of their own.

I also know there are people that will not like or understand what I am talking about. There will be people who do not believe any of my experiences and will be critical of all I have written. Maybe it is just too strange to grasp, too far out of their comfort zone or conflicts with their religious beliefs. That is okay, there are things in this life that I have a healthy level of skepticism toward. I was at a party not too long ago when one of the guests, an acquaintance in my immediate vicinity, asked me if I had seen any ghosts lately. The rest in our group exchanged looks with each other and had telling smirks on their lips. Along with that, they shared a giggle at my expense. I hesitated only because I half expected one of them to make an erie "woo" noise to be followed by more sideways glances and giggling. With comfortable ease, I said, "Yes as a matter of fact I have!" I was now the only one in the group with a grin on my face. I enjoyed that moment! I grinned because the spirit I had seen was in the house of one of the women in this group. I have since gotten a feeling from her that she is more open in her thinking. Trust me, there is more in this world than can be seen with your eyes.

My all time favorite story has to be the time I was in conversation with a person who had just recently found out about my gifts. As we talked, she proceeded to lean back from me as if I were contagious, like I had a "spirit seeing virus!" My gift is not contagious but I hope my enthusiasm for the subject is.

Welcome to my para"normal" life! I have only scratched the surface with a few of the reactions I have had from people. With a bit more time and subjection to me, the people around me will be more educated and less anxious about these topics. Personally, I can hardly wait for that day. I grow tired of people who would not dare to be or think differently from the next person. It is a risk to be different, lonely at times, too. I tried to be the sheep that followed blindly along to possibly blend in with the others. It did not work. Those that know me understand that there was never really a choice. I had to be true to myself and my God given gifts. I am at peace with my life and would not have wanted things to be any other way. I cannot imagine how bored and lonely I would have been without my spiritual visitors.

The next phase of finding my peace is that I have found my way to God through all of this. Very few people realize how truly spiritual I am. I keep God, in my own way, selfishly quiet. The final component, thus far in my journey to peacefulness, is the combining of God and my spirit world. In the beginning, these were two different realms. This journey has taught me that the soul goes on. Our body wears out or simply ceases to be and has its ending on this physical plane. Our soul or spirit continues on. For me, that place is called Heaven. I find that comforting and peaceful. In the end, I believe in me and in what I feel, see and hear. I believe my journey of personal and spiritual education is nowhere near completion. I say that with a smile on my face. I do not know that for sure, of course. Saying that, I feel, too, that this is my last trip back to Earth. I believe the remainder of my soul's education will come in spirit form. I look forward to each and every step yet to come in my blessed life. Thank you to all who have been a part of getting me to this point.

The rest is written, but yet to be experienced.

GLOSSARY

Apparition:

The appearance of a spirit in the form of a person, animal, or thing, which is visible to humans.

Clairaudient or Clear hearing:

The ability to hear voices, sounds, and/or music that is not audible to the normal ear.

Clairvoyant or Clear seeing:

The ability to perceive things that are not visible by everyone.

Cold Spots:

An area that feels colder than the area surrounding it. Some consider cold spots to be a sign of paranormal presence. It is thought spirits use energy from the surrounding area to manifest.

Crossing Over:

The belief that the soul continues on after the physical body ceases.

Empathetic:

Being sensitive to; the perceiving of or feeling directly the emotions of another person or group of people.

ESP/Extra Sensory Perception:

This is an ability to receive information that sensed with your mind; not through the recognized physical senses.

Ghost:

The spirit or soul of a dead person reflecting the appearance of their former living body but less substantial; a disembodied spirit form that appears among the living.

Gift:

Psychic abilities are often times viewed as a gift that comes from God. I view mine as being just that.Guardian

Angel:

An angel assigned to watch over and guide you, a particular person, or group.

Harry Houdini:

A famous magician who told his wife before his death that he would contact her after his death, if at all possible. (My aunt and I referred to this when she said she would come back to see me, if she could.)

Mist or Spectral Mist:

Is an energy field that looks like a cloud, mist, or haze. There may or may not be a certain shape or color to it. Thickness, density, and consistency might also vary.

Orb(s): Energy, spirit energy. Another theory is that energy is being transferred from a source, a battery, or_ power line, for example, to the spirit/orb for manifestation.

Ouija Board:

A flat board with the alphabet, numbers and other simple words such as yes and no printed on the surface. The game players put their fingertips on the edge of a pebble that is said to move about the board, after a question is asked, due to spirit or paranormal forces. The Ouija Board is also thought to be a portal for spirits to travel through.

Paranormal:

Events that happen outside the normal set of experiences.

Poltergeist:

A spirit that is considered troublesome because he/she or it moves things, chairs, car keys, etc. and is known to make noises, like knocking or banging.

Portal:

A doorway, gate, or any type of opening from one reality into another.

Psychic:

Someone who has an ability to perceive information not using the know senses.

Residual Haunt:

An event that repeatedly plays back a past event, like a recording playing over constantly. The spirit is not aware of the current day items around it, seeing only the way it was from its own era.

Prophetic Dreams:

(Also known as Precognitive Dreams.) Both are dreams of events before they occur.

Senses:

Refers to psychic senses. The ability to go beyond what everyone else can see, hear, feel, taste, or smell, beyond what even science can explain.

Sensitive:

The ability to feel information through extrasensory perception; susceptible to attitudes or feelings of others.

Shadow People:

Appear to be quite solid in silhouette, all black, do not reflect light, and have no discernible features other than the outline of the form. In our case friendly but moody.

Spirit:

A soul that did not pass into the light (for me, heaven) when the physical body died here on earth.

Spirit Energy:

Spirits need or use energy to manifest, appear on our physical plane.

Temperature Variations:

The theory that when a spirit is trying to manifest, the temperature will drop because the spirit is using the energy in that area to appear.

Made in the USA
Middletown, DE
14 August 2019